FAITH IN AN AGE OF FACT

Books by EDWARD H. REISNER

RELIGIOUS VALUES AND INTELLECTUAL CONSISTENCIES

NATIONALISM AND EDUCATION SINCE 1789

HISTORICAL FOUNDATIONS OF MODERN EDUCATION

FAITH IN AN AGE OF FACT

FAITH IN AN AGE
OF FACT

A New Religious Outlook

By EDWARD H. REISNER

FARRAR & RINEHART, *Incorporated*

New York   *Toronto*

Contents

FAITH IN AN AGE OF FACT

A New Religious Outlook

CHAPTER ONE

A New Religion in the Making

THERE are a great many persons in this present generation who have, as the orthodox preachers say, "lost their faith." And, singularly, these same lost souls seem neither to sense nor mind their desperate condition. They go about their daily tasks with optimism and determination. They govern their lives with moderation and sanity. They are active in good social works. They are apparently happy.

How can such things be? Are these men and women going on sheer nerve? Are they "putting on a front," while within they are lonesome and uncertain? Are they secretly longing for the security which was theirs in the old snug universe of their fathers, in which even the devils believed and trembled? Are they, perhaps, living on the increment of long ages of Christian tradition? Are they stealing a ride without making any contribution in the moving caravan of godliness and church activity?

Or is there an alternative interpretation of their apparent adjustment to life and reality? Is it possible that having "lost their faith," they have found a new one? That they have come upon new formulas of understanding and belief which serve as the framework of their sense of belonging, of moral direction and of eternal significance? That perhaps they are more, rather than less, sensitive to living moral values and more likely to see the true application of old moral concepts in the changing scene of contemporary life?

The second alternative is the one which is here accepted. There has undoubtedly come about a new orientation of the individual in the universe. It is a new universe, and in some sense a new individual, but there *is* a universe and the individual finds himself at home in it. He is one of its makers and builders.

The present undertaking to describe a new religious outlook which is in the making is not to be regarded as a project of private, personal invention or as a work of prophecy. On the contrary, it is almost entirely a job of reporting—a description of attitudes discoverable among the most intelligent and ethically sensitive members of this generation.

There may be some question as to whether the experience to be described is properly to be called religion. There will be those who would deny it that name and say that it is more accurately to be classified under the caption of philosophy. Undoubtedly the answer to this question will be an individual one and final decision should be left for later consideration. However, I should like to say that, in my opinion, the word religion is the only one which properly names the type of experience about which I am writing. It is religion, and not philosophy, because it represents the way in which men lay hold upon life rather than the way in which they provide intellectual explanations of phenomena.

The new religious orientation represents a logical extension and development of the Judaeo-Christian tradition. It bears somewhat the same relationship to modernism that modernism bears to fundamentalism. Modernism has departed substantially from the world view, the intellectual methods, and the ethical values of the earlier Christian tradition, but it has halted halfway in going modern. It accepts science up to a point, but it holds on to a considerable number of conceptions which are part and parcel of an intellectual system which is no longer authoritative—no longer even respectable.

The new religion is framed within a setting which is aggressively scientific. It departs even more radically than modernism from the historical intellectual setting, but at the same time it holds in large measure to the deeper spiritual insights and fundamental ethical values of the religious tradition of the Western World.

This new religion in the making is not to be thought of as one among the steady stream of new cults which are constantly coming to public notice and, in some cases, winning a large following. Christian Science, Dowieism, Bahaiism, Theosophy, and New Thought are examples of such, and a bit of looking back and about would bring to light many more. While these religious faiths differ largely among themselves, they are all, in one way or another, out of touch with the dominant intellectual habits of our times. In some instances they are built upon ignorance of history and science. For the most part they are feats in mysticism, offering ways of escape to the credulous or maladjusted.

On the contrary, the position to be developed in the following pages is that a religious change of first rate importance is already well advanced in the modern world. It is not here a matter of sects and cults, but of religion on the grand scale—of religion consistent with the authoritative intellectual canons of our day, cognizant of our best historical and scientific knowledge, and related in its ethical content to the structure and functions of our present society.

As against a widespread prepossession that no new formulation of religious outlook can take place in the modern scene, there are weighty considerations. Many of the great religions of the world originated not long ago as human time on the earth is considered. Compared with the estimated million years of the existence of man, the two and a half or three thousand years of the great classical religions is a short time indeed. Moreover, such religions as Confucianism, Taoism, Buddhism, Judaism, and Christianity originated within highly complicated and advanced societies. The intellectual progression to monotheism from the worship of many individual gods which took place not more than thirty-five hundred years ago, is in itself a sign of sophistication and respect for the demands of logic. Historical Christianity is an example of a religion which came into existence under mature ethical and philosophical auspices. While its titular founder was an unlearned man, the religion which went by his name and which he would have had difficulty in identifying as his own was formulated in the greatest center of scholarship of the Graeco-Roman world, in the midst of bustling commercial activities and in a preëminently cultivated society. Against such facts it will be hard to maintain the position that religious novelty can be expected only in ancient and primitive environments.

The contemporaneity and flexibility of religious experience are further supported from the history of Christianity itself. In the less than two thousand years of its history, Christianity has been many things. It has been changing constantly in response to surrounding intellectual and social conditions. The poetic religious insight and the way of the good life as set forth by Jesus differ almost to the point of contradiction from the metaphysical theology of the Nicene Creed of the fourth Christian century. The simple communism and the detachment from the world of the early Christian Church are in sharp contrast with the claim of the eleventh century popes to universal authority not only in the spiritual, but in the secular realm as well. The Christianity of the Middle Ages, accommodated to the feudal organization of society, is again very different from the Christianity which has been the sponsor of modern capitalism and of competitive nationalism.

Within the Christian faith much history has been written even in the last four hundred years. The Protestant Revolt is an example of fundamental change within the church. More significant still is the adjustment to the demands of science and historical research which has been steadily going on since the seventeenth century. Protestant Modernism represents a sensational departure from the intellectual positions of the Reformation period and even from those almost universally held in Protestant circles in the nineteenth century. New ethical values prompted by an awareness of the tensions of our industrial civilization and supported by a new conception of wholesome personality, are finding substantial acceptance within the Christian communion today.

We may well expect important changes in the comprehensive outlook of men and women in the contemporary world, because the present is a time of stupendous intellectual and ethical readjustment. The educated man has at last come to a matter-of-fact acceptance of the view of the physical universe and of life upon the earth which has been made mandatory by the scientific advances of the last century and a half. He has become committed to a description of mind which takes it out of the realm of metaphysical speculation and places it squarely within the network of natural phenomena. He has gained a degree of control over the material basis of human existence which invites a hitherto unknown optimism and suggests far-reaching, aggressive programs of human betterment. And during the last two centuries, and especially during the last few decades, there has matured for the sensitive individual a new sense of community which carries with it the restatement of ethical values and calls for a constructive attack upon the problems of political and economic organization. Such changes as these are so fundamental and so extensive that they have created a new man in a new world.

The present generation is in the strategic position of being the first to have lived long enough in that new world to feel at home in it. It is the first generation which has been able to develop toward that new world those patterns of adjustment and evaluation which may be called religious.

CHAPTER TWO

The Passing of an Intellectual System

MANY, probably most, of the changes which are taking place in the religious consciousness today are related to the disintegration of an intellectual system which has been so closely combined with the strictly religious experience as to seem inseparable from it.

The Christian world outlook resulted from a fusion of the Judaeo-Christian religion with philosophical systems which were authoritative in the cultural centers of the eastern Mediterranean during the early Christian centuries. Always excepting the materialistic ones, which obviously had little in common with the Judaeo-Christian world outlook, there are common characteristics among these philosophies which were adapted to Christian use and became the framework of the Christian religion. In all of them a separation is made between the guiding, controlling aspect of reality and the derived and dependent and inferior world of created things and human values. The first was eternal, changeless, perfect. The latter was characterized by its temporary and changing quality and by its imperfection. Absolute truth was a quality of that world which lay beyond human experience. Absolute good was discoverable only in the eternal pattern. Man's efforts to find truth and to be good could be at best only approximations of success.

In this system man occupied an interesting position. He possessed a rational faculty by means of which he was able to discover conceptual meanings. These humanly derived or experienced concepts were the same sort of reality as that which existed in perfect form outside of man's reach and above the scene of human existence. As man possessed the ability to think, in this respect and to this extent, he was godlike. At the same time his rational nature was inextricably bound up with the negative principle of matter—with those physical appetites and biological tensions which were in a constant state of conflict with his godlike self. To achieve the good life it was necessary to subordinate his bodily propensities to the demands of his rational part. The conception that man's rational faculty, or soul, was a part of the world of ideas, was the intellectual justification for a belief in its immortal existence. As part of the divine and eternal world of conceptual reality, the human soul was timeless. Its presence in a human body was only an incident in a life which transcended the world of experience and was eternal.

The Hebrew religion, and particularly the

Christian modification of that religion, came into the Graeco-Roman world at a time which was in some respects like our own. Educated men and women had lost their faith in the old religions. No longer could they take seriously the mythological explanation of natural processes nor the authority of merely traditional and customary morality. Their old world had fallen in ruins about them and they were desperately casting about for formulas of belief which would afford sanctions for tried and true virtues and at the same time be in keeping with the intellectual standards of the day. It was a period of active experimentation with new religious and philosophical systems. Epicureanism, Stoicism, and Neo-Platonism were among the philosophies which laid great emphasis upon a way of life and thus did double duty as philosophy and religion for many individuals of that time. During the same period religions from the Near East, such as Zoroastrianism, Judaism, and Christianity, made their bid for popular acceptance and were widely believed in and practiced. In addition there were many so-called "mysteries" of religious nature which emphasized purity of the individual life and bore the promise of eternal existence after death for their votaries. Out of this welter of conflicting and competing philosophies and religions Christianity emerged triumphant in the fourth century, and it did so because it was able in a preeminent degree to fulfill the religious needs of the age and at the same time to come to terms with the reigning intellectual fashion.

The monotheism of the Christian religion, which had been achieved at the end of a long process of religious evolution, was entirely consistent with the logical unity of the world which characterized the great Greek philosophical systems. The God of the Christian religion was easily identifiable with Aristotle's First Cause and Prime Mover, and with the universal Mind of the Stoics. In the first Christian century an Alexandrian Jew named Philo was able to restate the Jewish religion consistently with the demands of the Stoic philosophy. St. Paul, standing on Mars Hill in Athens, spoke to a crowd of the curious identifying the unknown God which they so ignorantly worshiped with the God of the Judaeo-Christian tradition. In support of his argument he quoted from the hymn of the Stoic Cleanthes the words, "in whom we live and move and have our being." The Gospel of St. John begins with a studied argument to the effect that Jesus represented the *Logos* of the Stoic philosophy, which was the abiding and effective spirit of reason as it operated in the world of nature and human society. "In the beginning was the *Logos* . . . and the *Logos* became flesh and dwelt among men." At the hands of Alexandrian scholars in the second and third Christian centuries the fusion of the Judaeo-Christian religion with the principal conceptions of Greek rationalism was convincingly accomplished, with the result of producing a religion embodying a theology which was little more than a restatement and adaptation of those philosophical positions.

The significance of this alliance which was accomplished between one of the great world religions and a particular system of philosophical thought may not be minimized. It was one of the most fateful unions for the subsequent history of the Western World which could be imagined. Up to that time the evolution of the God concept and of ethical values had taken place among the Hebrews on the easy basis of poetic insight and responsive to the changing circumstances of social life. From then on Christianity was a definitely bounded system, limited by formulas of abstract intellectualism which established standards of truth and goodness outside of the area of human experimentation. Moreover, Christianity had allied itself with a philosophical system which exhibited a steady and extreme disdain for man's biological functions. The philosophy provided the intellectual justification of the asceticism and withdrawal from the world which were strong characteristics of the early Christian centuries throughout the entire Mediterranean area. Given the spirit of the times, it is quite probable that these tendencies, as well as emphasis upon the compensations of the world to come, would have been present in Christianity quite independently of the sanctions of an intellectualistic philosophy, but it cannot be denied that the philosophy in itself encouraged that emphasis and afforded the means whereby a mood of pessimism regarding the earthly life became an essential and permanent part of Christian theology and religious experience.

Asceticism was not a significant part of the Jewish tradition and was only slightly manifested in the teachings of Jesus. Asceticism and withdrawal from the world were the practical counterpart of an intellectualistic philosophy. These attitudes and practices were taken over by Christianity and institutionalized as monasticism. The distinction between the worldly and the godly life deepened and hardened. The really good forsook the productive pursuits of the economic life. They abjured their civic responsibilities. They mutilated and starved their bodily nature for the greater glory of God. They denied themselves the sweet solace of family life as well as its responsibilities and opportunities. They foreswore the satisfactions of normal physical functioning. To be sure it was only the few who were strong enough to follow completely this distorted way of life, but the distinction between the higher and the lower, the better and the worse, was there and acknowledged. The everyday scene of falling in love and begetting children, of establishing family relationships, of doing the tasks of the workaday world, of functioning as citizens, of catching at passing opportunities for delight and laughter and recreation—all these were of the world and the devil, and not of God.

The development of the Judaeo-Christian tradition in the first thirteen centuries of the Christian era may in some sense be regarded as a detour of the human spirit. Nor did the organizing and interpreting efforts of Thomas Aquinas and other thirteenth century schoolmen contribute anything toward a recovery of true compass bearings. What they did was to restate, insofar as possible, Christian belief and practice as of the thirteenth century consistently with the philosophy of Aristotle, whose complete works had then but recently been recovered in Christendom. Nor did the Protestant Reformation, contrary to general uninformed belief, in any essential way disturb the statement of Christian philosophy as it had been prepared by Thomas Aquinas.

It is impossible in this connection to recount the story of the rising scepticism regarding the validity of the rationalizations of Christian philosophy which became more and more pronounced with the growing prevalence of the scientific temper

and the ever-extending conquests of scientific research. Suffice it to say that by the eighteenth century many thinkers had come to be thoroughly dubi-
ous regarding such generalizations as mind, matter,
God, and the soul, for which there was no warrant
provided in the testimony of sense experience. The
concept of matter, for example, which had been
taken more or less for granted, upon examination
showed decided vulnerability. Outside of the sensations which one gained of an object nothing positive
could be said of it. No one had ever experienced the
substratum of those sensations which had been so
easily assumed. The case, moreover, was no better
for mind, because as one looked within his experience nothing was discoverable there except some
sensation or its counterpart of memory. Just as in
the case of matter, over and above the particular
imagery which was experienceable at any time, there
was no entity or substance which could be identified
and named as mind. Scepticism regarding the individual mind or soul was easily transferable to the
theological concept of God.

The critical philosophy of Immanuel Kant,
given to the world in the second half of the eighteenth century, was a significant landmark in the
decline of the authority of the mode of thinking
which depended upon assumptions unverifiable in
experience. Kant was able to give good reasons for

the reliability of everyday experience and the procedures of science. At the same time he mercilessly exposed the unproved assumptions which were the stock in trade of rationalistic modes of thinking and demonstration. Once and for all he overthrew the towering structure of metaphysics which had been the stay and support of philosophy since the time of Aristotle and which had been so freely utilized in the construction of Christian theology. In this mighty fall went down the easy certainties by means of which philosophers had demonstrated the existence of the divine first cause and the immortal soul of man, which were the foundations of Christian theism.

For present consideration, one of the most important aspects of the intricate and extensive Kantian criticism lies in a series of puzzles which he discovered in human experience, of which one may be taken as an example. He found that human beings always demanded a cause for every effect. This universal expectation of a cause for every phenomenon called for a first cause of the cosmos as a whole. There before one's eyes was the world. Following common experience, the cosmic series of time and space relationships must have had a beginning, a first instance, an original occurrence, and since effects do not happen without causes, there must be found as explanation a first cause which was outside of and independent of the causal series of experience.

On the other hand, human experience just as obstinately denied the possibility of bringing that causal series to a conclusion. Go on back in time as far as you like and there must always be a "before." Get out to an imagined first end of the chain of happenings, and immediately experience presents a demand for a prior link. An insuperable difficulty arises in the fact that human experience simply cannot cut off the causal series at any point, but must continue to ask for and take for granted further extension of that series *ad infinitum.*

The impasse thus created could not be bridged by any argument which could be called scientific. As an offset to the right to expect experience to be orderly and reliable, one must accept the limitation that its processes and sanctions cannot apply beyond itself. The human reason cannot extend its jurisdiction beyond that experience which is initiated with sensations.

Kant explained the continuity of the individual's personal experience, but he made it seem useless to hope to discover within that experience the metaphysical entity known as the soul. He laid down a foundation for the secure use of the methods of natural science, but made it forever unjustifiable for men to apply the methods which were valid within experience to conceptions which transcended experience. In that realm in which scientific methods could be applied, one might always take for granted the presence of a cause for every effect and all of experience could be counted on as exhibiting cause and effect relationships. However, it was impossible to think of experience as a whole, as closed-in and completed, and then to go outside of this network of cause and effect relationships and posit the necessary existence of a first cause for the whole phenomenal world.

The critical philosophy of Immanuel Kant made a profound impression upon his generation and has conditioned all scientific and philosophical thought since his time. However, it must be said that the decline of the authority of rationalistic theology occurred less by reason of the work of philosophers than by the general extension and increased authority of scientific method and research. The positivist spirit won a resounding triumph with the publication of Charles Darwin's "Origin of Species" shortly after the middle of the nineteenth century. This work furnished indubitable proof of the changing character of organic species. When Darwin was able to show that species changed in the course of time and were not the eternal, immutable patterns of creation which Aristotle had considered them to be, the last prop of the rationalistic tradition was removed. An intellectual system which had been authoritative in the Western World for two thousand years and more had come to an end. The dominant mode of thinking of our day is realistic. It depends upon experience. It accepts the world as it is and refuses to take as its point of departure any unverifiable assumptions.

The question may well be raised whether in the absence of metaphysical systems there can be any long views of life and existence for the human individual. Is any satisfying personal orientation possible for the human being in the world which science describes? Can man have a sense of moral worth and significance when he sees himself as a part of a long process of biological evolution and his mind as a function of survival in his physical and social environment? When all those grandiloquent metaphysical formulas, which served for two thousand years to describe man's place in the world, have become empty and meaningless, is it possible that a human being may find for himself a sense of belonginess and a system of loyalties which will provide security and give direction to his individual existence?

Support for an affirmative answer to these questions is found in past human experience. Many of the great world systems of religion were created prior to and without the aid of metaphysical modes of thought. The Judaeo-Christian world outlook, to take the example most pertinent, reached a highly mature state before entering that phase in which it was profoundly influenced by the rigidities and false evaluations of classical Greek philosophy; and now that the Western World has gone through with and got over a long-enduring attack of intellectualism, man may come to independent terms with the universe which is the theater of his existence.

Such an adjustment will take place according to modes of experience which are poetical rather than scientific, intuitive rather than logical. That is not to say, however, that one's imagination operates independently of one's knowledge. Any world view which one may have will be unstable unless it be definitely related to and consistent with all that history and science and psychology have taught him. But, in the last analysis, he will more nearly follow the creative prophets and seers who looked into their minds and found there human values and purposes, than the speculative philosophers who have cut the stuff of reality into patterns all too neat and exact.

CHAPTER THREE

A New Framework for Human Values

THE twentieth century individual is committed to what the physical, biological, and social sciences tell him about the world he lives in. As he follows the revelations of astronomy his imagination gropes for a comprehension of distance in terms of millions of light years and of time told in billions of calendar years. He sees this earth in its cosmic perspective. With the physicist he has penetrated the constitution of the atom, and, for lack of better knowledge, he is content to accept the physicist's statement that all matter is ultimately reducible to electric charges. He knows that the constitution of matter throughout all space is the same and that the most distant star is composed of the same elements as are the things about him. Likewise he learns from the physicist the indestructibility of the elements of matter in spite of constant change and constant reorganization.

His point of view is also formed by the description of the earth with which geology provides him. He is at least familiar enough with the history of the earth to know the very great age of this planet and the more dramatic stages in its evolution to become the home of life. Geology and biology have prepared him for a realization of the gradual development of the myriad forms of living things which fill the pages of the earth's history and which occupy the scene of life today.

In his study of biology twentieth century man has observed the evolution of organic life from its simplest form to the most complicated. At one end of the scale he has seen the dawn of mind in the adjustment of unicellular organisms to their environment. From the single cell undifferentiated for receiving special stimuli and reacting to its environment as a unity, he has followed upward through the various phyla of animal life and has noted the progressive differentiation of organs for receiving stimuli and the increasing variety of response to those stimuli, mediated through corresponding adaptations of nerve structure. Finally, in the intricate nervous system of man he sees the anatomical counterpart of the most responsive and efficient psychological organization discoverable in any living animal. Mind, he is convinced, is an accompaniment of physiological structure and comes into existence only under certain favorable conditions and combinations of protoplasm. It is subject to the variations of the organism in connection with whose life it exists. In its manifestations from lowest to highest there is a discoverable continuity, and there is no reason for believing that the mind of man differs except in terms of more or less from the forms of mind discoverable in organisms beneath it in the scale of evolution.

The historical anthropologist has made clear the primitive origins of human life and the long struggle during a period of probably a million years in which mankind has come to its present condition. He has shown the slow accretion of material and social controls which mankind has elaborated to give it such commanding influence over the environment as is represented in the development of language, of the various vocational arts, of social institutions, of ethical attitudes and religious sanctions, and of art and recreational forms.

From specialized areas of historical and comparative study of human culture, the twentieth century man knows that the possession of religious attitudes and ethical values is varied in time and place and as the result of circumstance. Even the religious tradition of our Western World is seen to have had a history in which it progressed from relatively simple and primitive forms to later and higher forms. Its sacred book, the *Bible*, is recognized as the record of a long process of ethical and religious evolution. Christianity is seen to bear the stamp of social and intellectual environments and to have been many different things in the less than two thousand years of its existence.

Many individuals who accept the world which science has described for them, find that certain concepts which were significant enough in a more primitive picture of the universe, no longer possess meaning for them. One of these concepts so important for the older world view is that of a divine being who is the creator and sustainer of the world. Perhaps their difficulty lies less in accepting the idea of a creator than it does in the incomprehensibility of any process of creating something out of nothing. As students of physics they are aware that energy can fall from an active to a passive level and that matter takes various forms. However, they know very well that matter and energy cannot be annihilated. It is equally impossible for them to understand how matter and energy could be created. Furthermore the unfathomed extension of matter in space and the unimaginable antiquity of the organized and unorganized material substance filling space go beyond the conception of "a creation once for all."

Many who try to apply the analogies of everyday experience to the conception of creation become convinced that they do not fit. In the tidy universe of some centuries ago as seen by the unaided eye, it was conceivable that an all-powerful creator should have produced a round hot ball of sun with its planets and a great number of stars, but as the description of the sun has changed in the light of modern science it becomes unthinkable that any being could create that vortex of electric charges which is the sun or the endlessly spreading galaxies and nebulae which fill the lonesome ways of space. For them the search for a creator has become meaningless because the conception of a creation once and for all is not only beyond their imagination, but contrary to what they know of the nature of experienced reality.

Another concept which ceases to have any weight in the consciousness of many modern persons is that of a God who controls the operations of nature with reference to the well-being of this, that, or the other individual. The operations of nature are controlled within its own system, according to the attraction and repulsion of forces which only an infinite mathematics could describe. The idea of a manipulating providence is unthinkable. With the impossibility of intervention in the operation of natural forces any belief in miracles becomes untenable, because miracles are nothing more or less than the setting aside of the ordinary and expected operations of nature by a personal and willful choice on the part of a being in a position so to do.

A third idea which is likely to pass when one becomes committed to the scientific description of reality is that of an independent soul, or ego, which can continue its existence after physical dissolution occurs. Mind has been seen to be a function of a living organism. Its character and quality, its healthy manifestations, its efficiency, are related to the vitality and health of the organism as a whole. Many modern persons see no reason for believing that mind can exist independently of the organism in connection with which it has been manifested. Moreover they find no way of imagining any quality of mind if they attempt to imagine it separate from its body and no warrant for a belief in the separable identity or posthumous existence of the soul or ego.

Finally the man whose viewpoint has been formed in terms of modern science recognizes and affirms the reality of change. For him change is not illusion, nor is it the similitude of a process in which the elements of struggle and change are unreal because the outcome is assured in advance. The circumstances and conditions of today are not the same as those of yesterday, nor will the circumstances of tomorrow be the same as those of today. History never repeats itself and there is nothing old under the sun. Everything, from day to day, is unique and new. The fates of individuals and nations, of persons and institutions, are constantly at hazard. If desirable ends are to be achieved they must be planned for and sought for; they will not just come of themselves as aspects of the eternal constitution of things, willed in advance by a divine providence. Experience is not a treadmill in which the elements go through the motions of activity while all the time they are constrained by the invisible forces of an eternal, changeless, governing idea. Nor is experience the orderly march through time and space of the process of infinite evolution in which the end is known and foreseen and purposed from the beginning. On the contrary, experience is a questing, struggling, and creative process of change in time and space, in which the weight and force and relationship of the units involved are directive of the outcome. In human experience in particular, outcomes may be largely affected by factors of wish, purpose and determination.

I do not contend that in the preceding paragraphs I have described the way in which all scientific-minded persons look at reality, because I am aware of the fact that probably no two people do so exactly alike. I am satisfied if I have brought out clearly and provocatively, if you will, some of the more important characteristics of the scientific outlook of the present day, and if I have shown, beyond any possibility of doubt, that the world as revealed by science today is a very different world from that one in which the formulas of traditional and still operative religions found their intellectual setting.

There are many persons who do not see the possibility of any religious adjustment of the individual except in terms of those beliefs which it has been said are no longer tenable in the light of modern science. For such persons there can be no religion except on traditional terms. They would seem to hold that if one no longer believed in God as a Being existing outside of experience or experienceable reality, and in the human ego as a separable soul that may live on independently of the organism with which it had been associated in life, he could have no religion whatsoever. The only religion for which they would admit the name would appear to be one the tenets of which they could not accept. I hold that religion represents so varied and universal an adjustment of the human individual to the reality by which he is surrounded that it cannot be defined in such narrow terms.

CHAPTER FOUR

The Meaning of Religion

IT will probably be agreed that a mature religious experience is concerned with the most comprehensive orientation of the individual which is possible. Religion gives meaning to the individual's personal existence, not just in his relationship to his family, his business connections, or his social clique, but as a member of the entire human race, and not only in the present time, but in the historical past and in the distant future. It causes a man to view his actions not merely from the standpoint of their immediate consequences to himself or to a few individuals with whom he is in close contact, but in the light of their relationship to general conceptions of right and duty and goodness which have extensive application and long accepted sanction.

In the completely closed-in rationalistic systems which have furnished the intellectual setting for Western religion during the past two thousand years, the meaning of the individual's life was logically and definitively described in terms of a comprehensive and completed universe. The human being was given his position and meaning and function within that whole. In a naturalistic description of reality such logical precision can never be achieved. In connection with it we cannot use such terms as absolute, eternal, unchanging. However, if the religious orientation of the individual in a naturalistic world cannot encompass the outer fringes of a physical cosmos, it will at least place man in this awe-inspiring theater of action. If it cannot accept the specific terms of the Christian Epic in which man's entire history is told with complete certainty and assurance, it can at least project the moral purposes and strivings of the human individual against a million-year-long struggle for survival and happiness. If it cannot discover absolute and unchanging patterns of truth and goodness, it can at least chart the continuities which are discoverable in the process of social evolution and can identify the all but universal spread of certain ethical objectives as sought by sensitive human beings in the past and in the present.

It will probably also be agreed that religious experience involves the individual's sense of significance, of belonging, and of active partnership, and all these in the most comprehensive degree possible. What he does is worth something because it is a part of a great undertaking. His contribution of work and of loyalty is positively appraised, and thereby his life is saved from aimlessness and futility.

Also with reference to the larger purposes in

which the individual participates, it becomes possible for him to draw up a pattern of optimum selfhood. In the light of the whole, he learns what he as an individual ought to be and do. He is provided with standards of personal integrity,—with criteria whereby he passes judgment upon his personal actions and discriminates among various possible modes of conduct. He gains an ideal of constructive and courageous living whereby, high-heartedly and gallantly, he may meet the vicissitudes of fortune and, "having done all, to stand."

As a final quality of religious experience, it almost universally describes for the individual desirable modes of social activity. It gives him a social code, defining his proper relationships with his fellows and his proper attitudes towards them. But religion does more, much more, than lay down social codes. The historical religions are the original examples of "social planning." They present a program of social reconstruction,—an ideal picture of the ways in which men and women should live and work together. Religion enlists the human individual in the age-old and discouraging fight to bring into existence a more humane and happier community.

It is quite possible that others would wish to add items to this list of qualities and characteristics of the religious experience. Perhaps it might even be held that some of the qualities which are included above should not be. But at least there must be a measurable unanimity of assent to the meaning of religion as it has been defined. If it is possible for religious experience to exist and flourish in a world which is understood and described in terms of natural science, it will be expected to yield the same precious fruits of personal security and integrity, and of social service and loyalty as have been associated with the great historical religions of the past and the present.

CHAPTER FIVE

*Religious Experience Against the Intellectual
Background of Evolution*

B Y now it must be apparent that this is not an argument *against* religion. Rather it is asserted that religion is a natural and desirable aspect of an individual's total experience. Whatever his intellectual outlook, he finds need for placing himself as comprehensively as possible in the whole of things. Whatever his powers of self-analysis, he needs a conception of what he should be and how he should act. Whatever his tenacity in the pursuit of social purposes, his effectiveness is multiplied many times over when he is conscious of the age-old continuity of social ideals and when he feels the comradeship of countless human beings in the past and in the present working for common ends.

Having explored the changes in intellectual outlook which have occurred during the past two centuries, it seems desirable to present as clearly as possible the new religious orientation which is going forward within that new environment.

Very briefly the change may be described as one from a world outlook created through processes of

metaphysical speculation to one of complete acceptance of a world of actual experience. At the same
time, the change in intellectual methods involves a
shift from ethical values derived from conceptions
which lie beyond and are unverifiable in experience
to those which are discoverable within experience
and which undergo change and adjustment and refinement in relationship to factors of human need
and knowledge. It is difficult to understand the ob-
jections which are made when the frank proposal
is made to get along without the use of certain concepts which are the product of an outmoded
intellectual method. For after all there is no real
loss involved in accepting the widest possible orientation of the human being in his world that can take
place in the light of the intellectual canons which
dominate our generation. All the metaphysical systems which are or have been influential in the outlook of human beings are creations of human consciousness. All conceptions of divine beings, from
the simplest imaginings of primitive mankind to the
noble inspirations of prophet and seer, have welled
up out of the creative imagination of men. All ethical evaluations and ideals, from the simplest rules of
tribal conduct to the refined and universalized demands of the mature religious and ethical geniuses
of the race, are intertwined with actual circumstances
of economic and political organization and related to

the character and quality of community existence. The moral laws ascribed to divine beings have primarily been created within the individual and social experience of men and women. Mankind has made its gods ethical and changed the moral commands of those gods as certain human beings, individually and in groups, have gained new and higher insight into the ethical and institutional demands of a concrete social community. As has often been said before, men have created their gods in their own image.

Perhaps no better illustration can be found of the progressive moral development of a divine being in a changing network of human relations than is given us in the story of Jehovah's growth in the Old Testament. Here and there in its early pages one gets an echo of the fierce Bedouin code, as when Lamech declares that he will have vengeance upon his enemies to seventy times seven, or when Deborah celebrates Jael's murder of Sisera and the defeat of his forces. The ethical values that Jehovah favored in that earlier time originated in the moral practices and ideals of the Hebrew tribes and were easily and spontaneously transferred to him. At the beginning of the Old Testament narrative Jehovah was not even a tribal god, but only the patron divinity of a single family. His protection was over the members of the family and he brought them peace and plenty. They worshiped him at the sacrificial meal, pouring out his portion upon the sacred rock or smearing the sacred pillar with fat and oil. In morals, he was as easygoing as they, and accepted the crude and cruel nomadic code.

The laws promulgated by Moses at the Mount exhibit a distinct advance over the earlier moral standards of the Hebrews, and, accordingly, they represent God as ethicized to the same degree. By that time the exigencies of a more intricate group life had compelled and brought about a more involved and definite statement of mutual obligations and privileges within the tribe, although the members of the out-group remained as yet without moral status.

When wider political contacts and crushing national vicissitudes in the late centuries of the Two Kingdoms had caused the religious geniuses of that day to see the cosmopolitanism of virtue and the world sweep of moral values, the religion of the Hebrews came to possess its universal significance. Jehovah was recognized as the guide of all national destinies and not simply as the champion of a given race. His function was no longer to guarantee the success and sanctity of a single set of mores, but he was recognized as the commander-in-chief of all the forces of good everywhere in the world. If Jewish religion thus gained in universality, it gained no less in intensiveness. Each individual was to know his moral independence and his moral responsibility. Outward ceremonial gave way to inward experience. The fat of lambs and the blood of slain beasts were distasteful to a God who insisted upon the sacrifice of an humble and contrite spirit. Mercy and justice and humility were required of man, and only such manifestations of a regenerated and purified life were of worth in God's sight.

The mouthpieces and the creators of religious experience during this highest period of the Jewish religious development were the great spiritual innovators, Amos, Hosea, Isaiah, and others of scarcely less power. They studied the social and ethical conditions of their day and cried out against the greedy, swinish guilt of the orthodox followers of the reigning religion. Without hesitation they ascribed to Jehovah characteristics that were called for in their own application of the principles of ancient custom, but which had been lost in the formal application of law and rule, or voluntarily set aside. Of their own initiative they broke through the limitations of tribal ethics and extended wide the frontiers of the moral kingdom. "Are ye not as the children of the Ethiopians to me, oh children of Israel? saith Jehovah. Have not I brought up Israel out of the land of Egypt, and the Philistines from Caphtor and the Syrians from Kir?" The prophets recognized new ethical values, produced by changing political and social conditions, and they unhesitatingly spoke of them as the requirements of Jehovah for his people. They literally remade their God to include an intensive, spiritual, and universal morality.

The true succession of the Hebrew prophetical tradition occurs in the life and teachings of Jesus of Nazareth which represent the revolt of a truly religious and moral nature against legalism and class pride. Steeped in the writings of the great prophets of an earlier day, and possessed in himself of a spirituality that was adequate to the work of ethical and religious innovation, Jesus interpreted to his fellow men a new conception of God and of the higher life. He primarily conceived of God as the father of humanity. For him the human race represented a vast brotherhood, all sons of a common father, whom he recognized as the source and preserver of all ethical values. To be of God's kingdom would necessitate a state of mind of which the keynote is expansiveness of interest. If your life is to be one with God, to paraphrase the sayings of Jesus, exemplify in your dealings with your fellow men the same solicitude and love that God exhibits toward you. The universe is friendly to you; then should you also be friendly to men. Cleanse your heart of pride and self-satisfaction, becoming as a little child, and thus make room for the thoughts and actions that are of God's kingdom. Gain your own worth from the greatness of the cause you serve. Live in the lives and interests of others. Sow the seeds of altruism and reap the harvest of a richer, deeper soul life for yourself.

The evolution of religious and ethical experience among the Hebrew people as described in the pages of the *Bible* and recounted briefly above, is an outstanding illustration of the proposition that men make their gods after their own image. If one accepts this proposition, it then becomes necessary for him to reorganize fundamentally his outlook upon any particular religion which has developed historically, because his intellectual awareness has come to embrace the whole process of religious evolution. The religious consciousness is freed from any crippling adherence to any specific part of the entire record of the aspiring and groping of the human race. He gains a sense of the universal meaning of religion as he identifies it with the questing, upward-looking mind of man.

The present generation has been led behind the scene of God-making and ethical evolution. It has been compelled by the information brought to it by historical and comparative anthropology to recognize any accomplished religious formulations, whether of poetic myth-making or of philosophical rationalization, as having had their source in fundamental human needs and as having been channelled according to the circumstances of practical and intellectual environments. Our generation is sophisticated. Perhaps it knows too much for its comfort and happiness. Nevertheless it represents the continuation of the same human race which has been so actively and continuously engaged in the effort to describe, according to its light, the nature of the universe and man's place in that universe. It is only logical to suppose that new formulas of religious orientation will be sought and found which are consistent with the ruling methods of our intellectual life and which embody the deepest ethical insight of sensitive men and women in our generation.

In the religious consciousness of the modern man accomplished historical myths and rationalizations will find their setting in his awareness of the agelong process of ethical and religious evolution. His attention will be transferred from this, that and the other traditional formula, to the living, ongoing process. He will conceive his status as having shifted from that of unit in a finished whole to that of active participant in a growing world. His role will change from accepting a universe in which outcomes are predetermined, to assisting in bringing about changes which are desirable, but at the same time subject to the chance of failure.

The individual's identification of himself with the million year struggle of the human race for survival, safety, justice, liberty, and economic security, is a religious attitude of the highest order. To accept one's humble place in the human epic is a formula of individual orientation which is completely consistent with the dominant intellectual methods and findings of our generation. Moreover, this formula is not something which is here advanced only as a *possible* adjustment of the individual in long-range terms. This is not a proposal of something which *might serve* as a religion. On the contrary, it is a description of the way in which many educated and ethically sensitive individuals in our day actually find themselves looking out upon life and reality. The formula already has wide implicit or articulate acceptance. It is exemplified in the unconditioned, unmediated, independent enthusiasm of individuals for human betterment without reference to intellectual formularies, religious sanctions, or ulterior rewards. Moreover, for such persons their devotion to contemporary ethical objectives is not an isolated individual and temporary activity. It involves continuity with the long past and projection into the distant future. It rests upon a conscious comradeship with their human forbears who have contributed their bit to the processes of gaining control over nature, of organizing to better advantage social institutions, and of enriching human experience with forms of beauty and sentiment.

CHAPTER SIX

Man's Attitudes Toward the Physical Universe

AN examination of religious literature shows that manifestations of physical nature have from time immemorial filled the minds of men with experiences of reverence and awe and with a lively sense of dependence and advantage. The primitive man worshiped the soil which gave him food. He personified the rain-bringing clouds and the fructifying power of the sunlight. No less was he conscious of the destructive aspects of the natural environment, which threatened his existence and filled him with fear. His forms of worship were designed to keep nature and its beneficent aspects favorable to him and to propitiate those natural forces which could do him harm. Under primitive conditions of the arts and social organization the balance between the beneficent and the malevolent aspects of physical nature must have been extremely even, with the chances for survival very narrow. For such reasons the demonic aspects of primitive worship were perhaps more prominent than was the celebration of the kindness and goodness of the spirits which represented the friendly face of the physical world. This predominance of fear may still be seen in many primitive religions which survive into the present day.

In the religious literature which has come down to us, however, is to be seen a pattern of attitudes toward nature which is distinctly positive. Such expressions date back not more than four or five thousand years and they are an indication that by then man had brought nature under measurable control and found it coöperative with him in steady and reliable fashion. On this level of social and intellectual evolution, poets and seers celebrated the bounty of the physical world. The earthly theater of their existence was recognized by them as a decided asset.

Characteristically the beneficent aspects of the natural world upon which they depended were ascribed to divine beings. Before men had matured intellectually to the point of seeing the logical necessity of unifying all the processes of nature under a single God, they represented various aspects of the physical world as being the area of activity and control of separate divinities. The fruitful soil, the phases of seasonal change, the sun, the moon, the rain-bearing wind,—all these and many other particular aspects of the natural environment they deified. The happy circumstances of their existence were the result of the coöperation among the various divinities which controlled the natural environment.

When men were logically compelled to unify their experience of reality in terms of one supreme God, all the individual and various manifestations of nature were transferred to him.

On this last and highest plane of religious evolution, the one great God ruled nature, on the whole, to man's advantage. The cattle upon a thousand hills were his. The rains came in due season because he sent them. The thunderbolt and the earthquake were signs of his anger. Nature in its every aspect was under his control. Its beneficent phases, which happily were vastly predominant, were the signs of his pleasure and gracious approval. The earth was full of the glory of God and the firmament showed forth his handiwork.

There can be no doubt that human beings, operating on a prescientific plane of religious imagination, experienced a wide range of attitudes toward nature which were expressed in terms of the goodness and the power of God. The question immediately arises, however, whether in a scientific generation any attitudes which modern man may take in the face of nature can be called religious. Science has in large part taken the mystery out of the physical world. When the lightning bolt is the missile of Jove and the thunder is the voice of Jehovah there is much greater room for religious expression than when lightning is known to be an electric spark which finds its point of discharge according to physical laws, and when thunder is known to be the result of sudden heating and expansion of the atmosphere. Under modern conditions of scientific agriculture it is impossible to conceive of the worship of a baal, or soil god, because it is known that a crop depends upon specific conditions of soil and moisture. When a crop fails, instead of feeling that Baal has been unfavorable, one knows that the land needs bone fertilizer or barnyard manure, or that his agricultural project has been injured by an unusually low temperature or an amount of rainfall below that which is essential. Pestilence can no longer be regarded as a curse sent by God to punish men for their sins when one knows the bacillus which has been responsible for the disease and the agencies by means of which it is introduced into the human body.

In rebuttal, it must be said that the progress of modern science has only driven the mystery of physical nature farther back. For the naive wonder of the unscientific man in face of the gross phenomena of experience it has substituted the marvels, multiplied a hundred times, which the scientist discovers through his microscope, in his test tube, or at the end of a telescope. The universe described by Eddington and Jeans is far more mysterious and awe-inspiring than the cozy little playhouse of Greek mythology or Hebrew cosmology.

The only answer to the guarded caution of the scientist is to establish the difference between the detached, descriptive, intellectualistic experience on the one hand, and personal judgments of value on the other. The scientific description of what takes place in a field of growing corn is a very different thing from the value reactions of the farmer as he performs the operations connected with ploughing, planting, and reaping. The relief and satisfaction of one who greets a much-needed rain is a very different experience from that of the meteorologist who plots the course of moisture-bearing currents of air and who has successfully predicted the rainfall. The fundamental difference in question is the one between knowing and feeling. The astronomer may desist from his mathematical calculations to stand in awe before the majesty of the universe. The physiological chemist may conclude a research which has resulted in the discovery of the function of a certain hormone, to marvel at the intricate efficiency of human metabolism. And the biologist, immersed in the technicalities of an ecological survey, may sense the relentless, indomitable surge of vital energy. When a human individual makes for himself a judgment of personal value regarding the universe, he is operating in the field of emotion rather than in the field of intellect, although his emotional judgment may come as a response to the revelation which his intellectual proficiency has given to him. When all is said and done, the sophisticated intellectual of the twentieth century feels about the manifestations of nature much as his less learned ancestors did. No matter how educated a man is, he stands baffled before the mystery of the cosmos. Although he knows more about it than has any man in all the history of the human race, yet it remains for him as inscrutable a mystery as it was for any individual who lived in a prescientific age. Where did it come from? What is it coming to? How is it controlled? He has no answers for these questions. Furthermore, he cannot accept the relatively easy answers which less critical generations made. But there it is before him, and in its presence he is inarticulate and bows down with wonder and awe.

As the men of a simpler age looked at the intricate organization of living things and observed their adaptation to the environment around them, the whole thing seemed so wonderful that they said only God could have done this. From their experience of man's own contrivances they knew that stones do not come together to make a cathedral without the coöperation of human work and guidance. They knew that wheels and springs and plates do not assemble themselves to make a watch without a watchmaker. And so, following the demands of their experience, they said that there could be only one explanation, that this was a thing that had been planned and wrought by a divine being, who out of his infinite knowledge and power alone could do such work. The modern scientific man may not be able to say the name of God, but for the twentieth century successor to the nature-mystics of earlier intellectual eras the experience which called forth that name remains.

What, for example, can be more amazing than the economic and social organization of the ant? What can be more impressive than the story of organic evolution which shows the force of life creating organisms to take advantage of every opportunity for survival in the air, upon the earth and under the sea? And, finally, what is this which has produced man? What has brought into existence that complicated arrangement of protoplasm operating a chemical and physical process which the deepest researches of science have been unable fully to understand and describe? That combination of cells which has developed a lordly control over the forces of nature, which has produced music and poetry and various forms of plastic art, which has developed intricate systems of economic and political organization, and which has aspired to ethical ideals which transcend human accomplishment? In the last analysis it is not important what you *name* the force which is operating in this world and before which you stand in awestruck silence. The thing itself is what matters. The product is there before your eyes and you have characteristic religious attitudes in face of it, even though you hesitate to say the name which less cautious folk have used to make their meaning plain.

The question may well be raised whether the modern man can continue to regard nature as benevolent and friendly to his purposes. Particularly devastating to such an attitude is the conception of the struggle for survival of the fittest which is important in the theory of organic evolution. "Nature red in tooth and claw," unconcerned for the existence or the welfare of any individual or even of any species, is an unfavorable background for reverential or thankful attitudes. Will the human race or the insects finally possess the earth? Nature has no feeling in the matter. It simply provides the arena for a fair fight and no favors.

Charge against nature, however, all that you must on the score of the struggle for existence,— put in everything that must be included of cataclysm and disaster—and yet the resultant shows that the human race remains in nature's debt. Man's coming into existence and his survival through these million years were made possible only by the fact that the earth was a suitable home for him and responded in its bounty to his needs. If there had not been more of security than of harm, of success than of failure, of life than of death, the God of the Judaeo-Christian tradition could never have been created as a loving God. The dominant religion of the Western World would not be one of hope, but would be one of despair. Its deity would be a devil. It may confidently be asserted that no change in intellectual fashion can substantially alter the individual's reaction to nature as being benevolent to him and friendly to his purposes.

And, finally, no amount of scientific sophistication can take away from the twentieth century man the elevation of spirit which he finds in the beauty of his world. The distant mystery of the night sky, the chaste serenity of the moon seen through scudding clouds, the calm majesty of distant mountain peaks—all these stir the consciousness of every sensitive individual and cause him to say that they are good. It is as if there were a homing instinct within man which draws him back to love the beauty of the earth-mother who has brought him forth. Her beauty enters into him and sustains him.

It is not claimed that all individuals who find it impossible to accept a metaphysical structure within which religious values have been housed, experience the attitudes toward the physical universe which have been described in the preceding paragraphs, but it could just as truly be said that not all persons who are orthodox in their religious formularies would experience these attitudes either, in spite of the fact that the sacred literature of the religion which they profess exhibits them in great profusion. Sensitivity to physical nature is somewhat of an individual specialty. Thousands daily say, "Give us this day our daily bread," without realizing that in so doing they express their ultimate dependence upon nature for their survival and their comfort.

A factor which should be considered in this connection is the effect of urbanization upon the twentieth century man's awareness of the physical universe. City life to a considerable degree shuts the human being off from contact with nature. The moon and stars are obscured for him by the glaring arc lights overhead and in his daily work climatic conditions are important only as they may bring him some personal discomfort or perhaps interfere with his attendance at a baseball game. His dependence upon the bounty of the earth and ultimately upon the warmth of the sun remains for him obscure. The milkman, in some unknown manner, provides the daily supply of milk and cream. In the bins of the greengrocer is a never-ending supply of vegetables. The purchase of bread is a matter between himself and the baker. But he is oblivious to the way in which sun and rain and soil have cooperated with human effort to give him the food which keeps him alive and the materials which keep him clothed.

It cannot be a matter of indifference, as a factor of social health and coöperation, that these appreciations have been lost as a result of the twin processes of industrialization and urbanization. The continuation of our civilization and the recovery of healthy community life involve a rediscovery on the part of the teeming millions who dwell in our cities of their ultimate dependence upon nature and their responsibility not only for the conservation of natural resources but for the human labor which places at their disposal and use the necessities and luxuries of existence drawn from the earth.

There are many who have departed from the simpler form of the expression of faith, who remain obtuse, unsympathetic, and unresponsive in the face of nature. But it is here claimed that there is no reason why a change of intellectual fashion should in any important detail separate an individual from the great spiritual tradition of the Western World. Sensitiveness to the beauty of nature, awareness of his dependence upon soil and atmosphere and sun for the things which sustain his life, awe and reverence before the stupendous majesty and the orderly processes of celestial space, and baffled wonderment before the intricate structure and economy of living things,—all these may remain the possession of the modern man. Such characteristic reactions to the physical world represent a vital part of his total orientation to reality. If such attitudes have at any time properly been classified as religious, they remain so. And if it is possible for a man to have a religion outside of the traditional intellectual formularies of belief, the attitudes toward physical nature which have just been named, may well be found to be a part of it.

CHAPTER SEVEN

Man as Member of the Human Family

I T is easy to see from a historical and comparative study of religion that man's relationship
to the society in which he lives has always been
a subject of religious interest and invention. Primitive tribes commonly revere their ancestors as divine
beings and even such advanced religions as those of
the Greeks and Romans found places in their
pantheons for the reputed founders of their races
and political organizations. As has been indicated in
an earlier connection, the religion of the Jews was
throughout its entire course of evolution based upon
the conception that Jehovah was the God of the
Hebrew people. The social institutions of the Jews
were regarded as having arisen from divine command and any failure to live up to them was to be
regarded as disloyalty to the real head of the people.
The history of modern and contemporary govern-
ments likewise indicates a close relationship between
social institutions and religious sanction.

This practically universal recognition that
man's social relationships possess religious significance leads us to expect to find in man's social rela-

tionships today and under new intellectual auspices, an area in which the religious experience is to be found. If modern religion involves certain comprehensive adjustments of the individual to the physical universe in which he lives, just so it may be expected to find a place for the orientation of the individual to the long past of the human family and to current forms of social organization.

Historical Christianity undeniably has exhibited social reference and possessed a social philosophy, but when one examines it with reference to its social implications it shows a deep-seated ambiguity. On the one hand it invokes attitudes of friendliness and coöperation. It represents all human beings as sons of a common father and therefore brothers. It enjoins upon each thoroughgoing respect for the personality of all others and establishes service to others as the fundamental spring of individual action. Christianity is essentially a social philosophy of philanthropy, equality, and mutual coöperation. It represents democracy. Its social principles could be, and of necessity must be, the foundation of significant family and community life. They could provide sufficient motivation for the humanizing of all institutional arrangements within any given nation and for the establishment of peaceful coöperative relationships among the nations of the world.

On the other hand, Christianity in its original

statement was a philosophy of political and economic
defeatism. It was a philosophy of life set forth by a
Jew at a time when Jewish independence had been
lost, and when the individual Jew was no longer
able to participate in the functions of citizenship. It
was a religion of political escape. To Jesus the possibility of a reëstablished Jewish nation seemed hope-
less and his gospel was a way of life for a mutilated
and partial human being who could no longer hope
to function as one possessing civic rights and duties.
For his Jewish contemporaries he described an ideal
of conduct without reference to civic functions.
"Render unto Caesar the things that are Caesar's,"
he said, "and to God the things that are God's."

Jesus' conception of the economic functions of
the individual was equally negative. In the spirit of
the oriental holy man he told his followers to take
no thought of what they should eat or what they
should put on because God fed the sparrows and
would take care of them as well. He counselled the
rich young ruler to sell all that he had and give his
possessions to the poor. All ordinary economic activities were to be forsaken because they operated
against the full expression of the spiritual life. In
somewhat the same way he saw family relationships
as interfering with full religious expression. He told
his disciples to leave father and mother and all en-

tangling family relationships and follow him in a life of full religious devotion.

Obviously the counsels of Jesus on economic and family life have never been followed in Christendom, for if followed out to their logical consistency they could mean nothing short of the destruction of human society. The very existence of a social order implies political administration, the production and distribution of the necessities of life, as well as some system of family organization. Christendom has never been Christian in the sense that it has followed the teachings of Christ in their full implications. What is more, Christendom could not have endured and no human society could endure following the strict and literal application of certain aspects of the teachings of Christ. What sharper contrast with the social axioms of the humble carpenter of Nazareth could be found than the wealth and power and pride of the Church from the eleventh to the thirteenth century? And what more complete antithesis to his economic philosophy could be found than the preoccupation with wealth and the glorification of the virtues which brought wealth which have dominated the religious expression of modern capitalism?

If the Christian church in its middle history recognized the way of withdrawal from worldly life as the better, yet it did not desert the mundane con-

cerns of men entirely. It made an effort to bring into
everyday relationships as much of the spirit of Christianity as was possible. It set up and endeavored to
enforce an ideal of mutual service among the classes
of feudal society. Into all political and economic relationships it attempted to infuse, according to
mediaeval standards, the spirit of justice and
brotherhood.

Organized religion in the Western World became sponsor to a set of social institutions created
during the time of the Church's most complete
ascendency. Its prerogatives and powers were built
up and sustained, first within the structure of feudal-
ism and later within that of absolute monarchy in
the developing nation-states. While it has adjusted
itself gradually to changing social circumstances, the
Church has consistently been the defender of existing institutions and of the social *status quo*. It has
generally been the opponent of novelties of social
philosophy and of social reorganization.

The lines of conflict between traditional religion, joined with vested social interests on the one
hand, and forces of social innovation were clearly
drawn in the second half of the eighteenth century.
At that time there came into the stream of European
opinion a body of new and revolutionary social ideas,
which, because they are essentially the ruling social

conceptions of our own day, deserve more extended consideration.

Instead of accepting existing social institutions as something sacrosanct and God-given, the new social philosophy considered social institutions simply to be serviceable ways of ordering social life, developing in response to specific social conditions. As social conditions change, old institutional forms tend to become in some degree misfits. Accordingly they should be subject to constant overhauling and readjustment.

Eighteenth century reformers saw the desirable way to secure changes in laws and political institutions in the provision of a lawmaking body, the representatives of which were to be elected by the people. The most extreme interpretation of the basis of suffrage was to give every adult male, irrespective of his wealth, a voice in the selection of representatives. This extreme liberality with respect to the right to vote was not, however, a dominant note of the eighteenth century social philosophy. It was only in the nineteenth century that the more progressive nations of the Western World went so far as to include in their conception of representative government the right of the propertyless class to take part in the management of social concerns.

The new eighteenth century social philosophy included also a sense of obligation to improve the lot of the working masses. The common people, of whom there were many, performed the social functions which insured the comfort and security of the upper classes, who were few in number. Something should be done, it was held, to relieve the ignorance, the poverty, the insecurity, and the anxiety of the most numerous portion of society. Society must be reorganized so as to eliminate insofar as was possible the heartless exploitation of the masses, and a new social algebra was to be put into operation which would count every human being as one and by means of which would be worked out the equation of the greatest happiness of the greatest number.

Perhaps the most significant characteristic of that new social attitude was its optimism. Gone was the fatalistic acceptance of the world as God had made it. If the earlier social outlook had taken refuge in the promise that the rewards of an after-life would even up the discrepancies of a short sojourn in the vale of tears, the new social philosophy declared an attack upon poverty, illness, war, injustice, and social oppression. Whatever the promise of the future life, there was no reason why this life should be so full of unhappiness and frustration for the great majority of human beings.

All these new social attitudes taken together constituted a revolutionary conception of the nature of a social community. Reinterpreted in terms of the new social ideal, the nation-state, which was then the dominant form of social organization, was to be regarded as an adventure in human welfare. Each citizen was expected to coöperate toward the good of all and the function of the political state was to bring about optimum conditions for the happiness and welfare of its citizens.

Naturally enough the new social ideal of the eighteenth century was not realized at once. After a century and a half it has not been realized except in small part in the world today. But the ideal has not perished. It has grown with each decade and with each generation and today remains the constructive social ideal of morally sensitive and earnest men and women.

The word to which the eighteenth century social philosophers attached this new conception of human society was progress. Many of the inventive minds of that period believed that the human race had come from distinctly unfavorable conditions to those that were relatively favorable and that the future saw vast possibilities of improving the lot of mortals. Each new generation, applying scientific knowledge in the interest of human welfare and improving human institutions through more equitable laws, could thus create better conditions for the development of a better younger group, who in turn with a superior start would carry still further the improvement of institutional life. For these men human improvement was a fundamental objective. They devoted their individual lives to this cause. Their energies were harnessed for pulling humanity upward. They were not detached from their kind, they were in and of the human race, concerned with its fortunes, committed to its improvement, and devoted to the extension of human happiness and good. It might be added, for them this social philosophy was a religion.

In this connection, as we are discussing the development of what may be described as a distinctively modern view of social ethics, it seems desirable to call attention to the positions of Absolute Idealism, a philosophy which dominated a considerable portion of the intellectual world of Europe and America during the last decade of the eighteenth century and the first three of the nineteenth. The Absolute Idealists introduced into their world view the conceptions of evolution and immanence. In other words, they held that God was progressively realizing himself and that he was doing so in terms of and by means of the actual physical world and the historical development of mankind. For this philosophy God was not a being outside of the world who had created it and who exemplified in his own nature perfect canons of truth and goodness which were set up for the guidance of mankind. The absolute idealists saw man and man's institutional life as the essential moral self-expression of God. The only morality which the absolute could experience was the morality of human beings. The only good there was in the universe was the good which had been created in individual moral effort, and all the moral striving of mankind summed up to represent the moral nature of the absolute. The efforts of moral self-realization of the absolute were at once expressed and found in social institutions and with every new concept of social justice and humaneness, God grew in moral stature. Man's social expression was of the very reality of the absolute. Man's economic life, his political organizations and all of his other social manifestations were of the essence of reality. The individual man was a partner of the absolute in the great adventure of moral self-realization.

The scientific-minded person of the twentieth century will find it impossible to accept the metaphysics of Absolute Idealism and he may well be chary of accepting some of the social rigidities which it tended to justify and sanction. But disallowing all of the cobweb connections spun by the metaphysical imagination of the Idealists around the realities of social existence, there is a residue of social outlook which remains impressive even to the scientific temper of our day. The moral significance and the tremendous drama of human history remain basically real and the individual's connection with the upward march of mankind seems inescapable. The human individual of this generation may truly see himself as a responsible participant in the human epic. In terms of practical economic control over nature, of the improvement of political institutions, of the enhancement of human liberty, of the extension of scientific knowledge and method, of the development of literature and art, of the refinement of moral values,—in terms of all these the individual man of the present-day is debtor to all of mankind who have preceded him. He is the heir to all the advantage which human striving has produced. He is the beneficiary of a system of moral effort which extends backward in an unbroken line to the first emergence of mankind out of his prehuman ancestry, and if one is to be logical there is no reason why the continuity should not be extended backward still farther into the beginnings of life itself. Human science has not yet been able to bridge the gap between living things and inorganic matter, but is there any reason to suppose that the continuity which accounts for man as he is does not extend still farther back into the constitution of the inorganic world? Man is a part of reality and man's moral striving is likewise a part of reality. The moral nature of man is of the stuff of which the world is made.

As the sensitive human individual feels at his back the serried lines of countless generations, he faces forward to do his bit in achieving a higher destiny for the human race. As a maker of economic goods, as an actor in political administration, as a member of a family circle, and as a participant in the informal social activities of rest and play, he is creating reality. Moreover, he is determining the direction in which the life of mankind shall move. He is not an isolated self. He is not a detached individual. He is an associate, a comrade, in the enterprise of human living and world improvement. His objective is that men may have life and may have it more abundantly. His concern with human institutions is that they shall foster human welfare ever more and more adequately. It is his essential business to participate in the creation of a community of "all for one and one for all."

In exploring the relationship of the individual man to the human family we have been led to accept a social ethic which takes as its goal the realization of the ideal community, in which the welfare of each is the interest of all. This conclusion has not been arrived at through processes of logical proof. Rather it has been a matter of reporting man's ethical aspirations. The position accepted is not new. As has been pointed out above, it has appeared in primitive social organizations and in those aspects of primitive religion which deal with social relationships. It is discoverable in many of the great world religions. It runs through the entire history of Judaeo-Christianity. Indeed the ideal has never had more noble expression than in the inspired utterances of the prophets of the Old Testament. Its fundamental teachings are those of the carpenter of Nazareth and it is the refrain of noble and sensitive souls throughout the whole course of modern history.

In certain respects, however, this old ideal receives a new expression in our modern times. The control over natural phenomena which man has gained in these recent centuries through his knowledge of science introduces a new element. This is found in the proposal to utilize in a constructive way the new economic possibilities of a technological civilization for creating security and raising the standards of living for all. No longer does man turn away from the social scene in despair. He sees the possibility of utilizing economic forces for the realization of the good life. He also possesses the dream of political organization and activity which accepts as its objective the remaking of social institutions in terms of the general good.

The ideal of a coöperative community is still far from being realized in any part of the world today, but at least there *is* an ideal which serves as the blueprint of a new and better community life.

CHAPTER EIGHT

A Positive Appraisal of Personality

IN no area of experience does the acceptance of a naturalistic outlook impel more thoroughgoing reorientation than in the appraisal of human nature.

The traditional Christian view of personality irredeemably split up the individual. Christian metaphysics posited a sharp division between mind and matter. Even in the mind there was a higher and lower, and it was only man's rational faculty which possessed a full positive evaluation. Human reason was the only godlike part of man. It alone participated in divine reality. It was the factor which marked man off from brute creation. It was the window of the soul which opened outward to God. All other mental faculties except reason were subsidiary and inferior. The senses, by contrast, opened toward the material world. They were the sluiceways through which physical appetites and biological urges threatened to flood and engulf the citadel of reason. The natural tendencies of the human will were but mental manifestations of the devil's realm and of his power.

The traditional Christian view of human nature was one of extreme pessimism. According to the Christian ethic

> "In Adam's Fall
> We sinned all"

as stated in the pages of *The New England Primer*. Man was born to sin. "For all that is in the world, the lust of the flesh, and the lust of the eye, and the pride of life, is not of the Father, but is of the world." Man was a "broken reed," "a worm in the dust," "an unworthy vessel," "a brand plucked from the burning." In the good Christian home from his tenderest years the child was impressed with his sinfulness and need of salvation, and a sense of guilt and personal inadequacy followed him through maturity into old age, even to the brink of the grave.

A naturalistic appraisal of the human individual stands with reference to the traditional Christian one as do the opposite poles of a magnetic field to each other. According to the former, the human individual is a unitary organism. His mind is essentially and inextricably related to his physical body. There is no separation as of higher and lower between his processes of thought and the processes of sensation, memory, and imagination. Thinking takes place by means of images and ideas and is invoked when practical situations call for novel adjustments.

Mental health and proficiency are directly dependent upon or related to nervous structure. Brain lesions or defective nervous systems are reflected in mental disability. Mental proficiency is influenced by bodily states. Emotional tones are the echoes of the sounding board of the physiological structure. Metabolic harmony depends on mental health.

It is impossible in this connection to more than hint at the marvelous miracle of the human organism. The human being is originally a single cell compounded out of potentialities for future development which are gathered out of the genes of his parents, grandparents, and more remote ancestors. The immature pattern of the individual-to-be makes use of the materials provided by its mother-host and builds itself. This self is made up of living cells combined in marvelous ways for the creation of an independent organism which can live on its own, adjust itself to a world of men and things, and participate in creative activity. The outstanding characteristic of the human individual is that, while immature and undeveloped, he possesses the power to appropriate in the course of his maturing the previous experience of the human race. He grows up into and is at home in a culture which has been a million years in the making. The human infant acquires and uses language. He takes over for his own use in easy stride the practical skills and the

controls of nature which have been laboriously accu-
mulated in the history of mankind. He enters upon
an inheritance of science and art. He naturally and
easily falls into the social arrangements and the
system of moral values which govern the community
within which his lot is cast. The human individual
is in sober truth the "heir of all the ages." He is not,
however, only the heir. He is the steward and the
extender of his patrimony.

One tends to overlook the fact that human experience is as much a part of reality as are the more
material aspects with which it is likely to be con-
trasted. The human beings who have adapted fire
to their needs, constructed dwellings, domesticated
cattle, cultivated fields, navigated water, developed
a religious outlook, written poetry and drawn pic-
tures, established social institutions and decreed
moral values, and discovered those continuities and
regularities of nature which go by the name of
science,—all these have played a part in the creation
of reality. Indeed, the experience of mankind is a
unique and superlative form of reality and nothing
in all nature is more godlike and divine than the
creative, forward thrust of human experience. If the
sixteenth century astronomer Kepler could exclaim
in rapture as he viewed the beautiful mathematical
precision of movement of the heavenly bodies, "I
think God's thoughts after him," one might equally

well say upon gaining a true perspective of human experience, "I see the continuing act of creation."

Perhaps the human individual, from his prejudiced viewpoint, might not be justified in saying that human personality and the creation of experience which is carried on through human personality are the most precious things in the universe, but certainly it can be said that human personality is tied up with the most intricate organization of matter which is discoverable in the world today. Human personality possesses more of freedom, of independence, of initiative, of invention, than anything else to be found in the heavens or upon the earth. Human personality is a precious thing.

The Christian tradition, it is true, placed a positive estimation upon the human individual, but it centered its regard upon a theoretically perfect aspect of the human being, namely, his rational nature, while placing a negative evaluation upon everything else which was a part of him. As has been said above, the newer and at present authoritative modes of describing man's mental life refuse to accept such a dualism as this. Our day sees the human individual as a <u>unity.</u> The physical frame of the person, the sustaining and governing physiological processes, the deep-seated, automatic, biological urges, the intellectual processes, emotional reverberations, practical activities, and moral aspirations,

—all these are necessary and contributing parts of the organic whole which is a human personality.

The differences between the ways of viewing the human individual just stated are definitely reflected in contrasting systems of moral evaluation. The older outlook was much concerned with the salvation of the individual's soul, which was the *& body* eternal, immaterial, and spiritual part of him. The soul was the thing that mattered and it was essentially abstracted from the complete circle of human self-expression. The whole man was at war with this special part of himself. It was thought that the soul's welfare was best assured by the suppression of other aspects of the whole individual. To save that soul was the chief objective of ecclesiastical administration and of man's striving on earth. The newer outlook regarding the ends to be achieved in connection with the individual life is very different. It sets up an ideal of wholeness, of efficient self-management, of happiness, and of rich and varied self-expression. The new concern is not so much with saving souls as with building happy, efficient, creative personalities.

If a positive evaluation of personality is one of the fundamental positions of the new religion, it seems desirable that we should attempt to outline some of the conditions and characteristics of optimum selfhood. The foundation of good personality is a sound body. It is possible for a person to rise above physical weakness, pain, and ill-health, but it is difficult and rare. There is no greater single good in life than to be healthy and vigorous, to greet each new day with the enthusiasm born of steady strength, to do the work of that day on a sustaining reserve, and to look back upon its accomplishment from a state of normal fatigue which still leaves room for enjoyable relaxation and rest. The body is the powerhouse of individual achievement. It should be operating at a point of utmost efficiency.

The appetites are the natural purveyors of the fuel which keeps the powerhouse going, and it is the individual's responsibility to manage his appetites to the best interests of his entire personality.

Among the instrumentalities of normal functioning is sex. In every range of life, nature is preeminently interested in continuity and has provided for the reproduction of the individual and the species as one of its first concerns. Accordingly the sex instinct in all forms of animal life has been made one of the most imperious of all biological drives, and this is just as true of man as it is of any of the other orders of animal creation. Sex is fundamentally related to the entire process of the individual's growth, maturity, and decline. It is intimately connected with the proper balance of metabolic processes. It governs emotional poise. Both its expression and its sublimation are inescapably connected with the more ideal expression of human activity and aspiration. Misdirection and misuse of the function of sex are among the potent forces of personal unhappiness and moral collapse, while the proper manifestations of sex life are substantial aids in the development of happy, serene, and integrated personality.

It is a fundamental position of the new world outlook that we should reverence the physical body. In the words of Robert Browning,

"Nor soul helps flesh more, now, than flesh helps soul."

However important for the fullness of personal life good bodily health is, that alone is not enough to make a personality. It is a commonplace that there are many little, frustrated, split-up, misdirected, unfruitful persons who inhabit sound bodies and enjoy excellent health. It is equally trite to recall the fact that there are many great persons who have risen above physical weakness, ill-health, and outright deformity to make important contributions to the world's treasury of good deeds and noble thoughts. The ideas which a man has, the organization and arrangement of those ideas, the moral values which he prizes most, the discipline which he is able to impose upon himself, the activities into which those ideas extend themselves,—these are the things that really make the person.

Character is partly a matter of the pattern of ideas and partly a matter of executive habits. Perhaps a more acute psychological analysis would transfer much of habit over into the realm of ideas, but all of us are aware of the practical distinction between the ideational and the doing aspect of conduct. So often we know the better and do the worse. Some individuals much more easily than others grow weary in well-doing. There is a great difference in the decisiveness and persistency of individuals in action. But certainly both the furnishing of the mind with a system of ideas which carry with them conduct values as well as the strengthening of the executive aspect of conduct are involved in character education.

Character education is the biggest part of all education. "What a man thinketh in his heart, that he is." If education is a matter of making and forming men and women, its chief interest is in outcomes of character. The scope of character education is so broad that it involves the whole texture of experience,—the experience which a child receives through the more informal agencies of the community environment, the experiences which he acquires in the home, and finally those experiences which the school, as the formal educational agency of the state, provides for him.

Some attention deserves to be given in this connection to personality adjustment in a more specific sense. It is only in recent years that the advances of psychiatry have called attention to the immense human loss which is sustained on account of the ineptitude which individuals exhibit in the management of their lives. Many weaknesses and failings of personality have been identified and described. There are individuals who suffer from a sense of personal inferiority. There are others who take refuge in wish-fulfillment rather than in practical performance. There are those who excuse their weaknesses in terms that place even their failures in happy light. There are many whose minds are possessed by fears and hates. And so on we might extend the list of failures in personal management and self direction.

By contrast with this pathology of personality a pattern of healthy wholeness might be shown. The wholesome personality makes an objective, accurate appraisal of himself, knows what he can do and what he cannot do, takes positive satisfaction in the proficiencies of which he is master and does not allow himself to bewail the lack of capacities which others possess and he does not. On this basis of objective self-appraisal he eliminates jealousy from his life and is able to take pleasure in the accomplishments of others.

The healthy personality is also honest with

himself. He does not manufacture excuses of self-justification for his shortcomings. He does not allow a personal loss or an emotional disturbance to dig in and protect itself and from this vantage point expand like a malignant growth to touch and influence every aspect of his experience. In the most general sense of that word, the healthy-minded person is not selfish. Whether he be poet, creative artist, or philosopher, or engaged in overt, objective dealings with men and things, the direction of his life force will be outward rather than inward. He will point his actions and interests away from ingrowing preoccupation with himself.

Good self-management is something which may be achieved, and such achievement represents one of the substantial values of human existence.

The overt and positive expression of selfhood is the work which the individual does. The part which a man or woman plays in the everyday world, in the production of food or the means of clothing and shelter, in the making of a home which fosters growing life, in the marts of commerce and trade, in the scientist's laboratory or the philosopher's study, in the schoolroom or on the stage,—whatever a man or a woman does to maintain and further the life of society and the operation of social institutions,—that is his or her main business and the principal expression of his or her personality.

In an earlier connection, when discussing the attitude which some modern men and women have taken toward human society, it was said that one could not hold to any other than a positive view of the various aspects of institutional life. In the appraisal of personality, socially useful work is regarded from the standpoint of the man who performs that work. It is necessary to take a positive attitude toward the activities of the individual producer as well as toward the social product which he creates. It is the tragedy of any society when the best which a man has to give is thrown back into his face as unesteemed or unwanted. When large numbers of persons are doing underpaid work, wasted work, trivial work, work which is deemed low and menial, we have sure proof that the economic institutions of that society need revamping. In any society which is organized with reference to the needs of the individuals which compose it, no honest work can go unrewarded and no honest work can be disesteemed. A man's and a woman's work is the best that there is within them. It is their principal contribution to the ongoing stream of human experience. It is a creative, godlike exercise of function and as such it should be reverenced.

It is an anomaly and defect of our civilization that man's labor is so exclusively regarded as a commodity, something for sale and all too frequently something which is sold extremely cheap, or to which there are attached meretricious and accidental values which produce shocking disparity in reward. Under our present economic order there seems to be no way to avoid the money evaluation of labor, but much remains that can be done to lessen the injustices in the rewards of labor, to restore the laborer's self-respect and pride in his job, as well as to express the concern of the entire social community for the security and the welfare of those whose labor provides the material basis of our civilization. A primitive age of human culture was more just in its evaluation of the meaning of labor than is our sophisticated age. Early cultures appreciated the significance of the farmer, of the smith, of the builder, of the herdsman and the sailor, for they represented those branches of human activity as presided over by gods and goddesses. It is no less true now than then that the daily productive labors of men and women are not only touched with a religious interest, but represent the highest of human values.

Still another aspect of human personality which deserves high estimation is comprised in those pursuits which furnish relaxation. Any organism has recurrent periods of work and rest. For good functioning the latter are just as important as the former. The leisure time pursuits of the individual, the things he does for rest and recreation, deserve positive evaluation.

The Judaeo-Christian tradition has, on the whole, done injustice to the lighter side of human nature. It has been dead serious all the way. It has stressed holiness too much and happy good times too little. Its God is seen as angry, as kind and compassionate, as stern and judicial, but never as laughing. The Puritan tradition which has so completely dominated the later phases of Christian evolution, has been especially negative in its estimation of the lighter side of human life. According to that tradition, things were considered to be wrong because men liked to do them. The Puritans seemed to go out with the intention of deliberately stamping out all manifestations of pleasure. In many Protestant churches in the United States today the catalogue of things which the godly person may not do is so long and inclusive as to eliminate practically all opportunity for group sociability. To be sure, the Puritan ideal was so false that it could not be lived up to. Human beings under that system found opportunity for relaxation even though they did so with a feeling of guilt.

Now any sensible person knows that the strictly ascetic life represents a distortion of human personality. Laughter is just as natural as tears. Play is as holy as work, or perhaps it is better to say that neither is particularly holy, but both are natural and worthy of positive evaluation.

Why should we not sing praises of lightness, of laughter, and of relaxation from work? The man to back for the long run is the one who knows how to relax at times. The sound personality is not always strung up tight. The preternaturally tense person, the person who works beyond the just limitations of his strength, the person who can never unbend to play or to enjoy some recreational form of beauty, is likely sooner or later to crack. Let us find a place in the sanctuary of human values for laughter, for games, for the rich enjoyment of various forms of aesthetic expression, and for wholesome simple rest.

CHAPTER NINE

The Nature of Evil

THE problem of evil banks so large in the religious consciousness that it is desirable to see what disposition of it may be made as part of a naturalistic outlook upon the world and life. Thoughtful persons have always been led to seek an explanation for the evil which besets human existence. The Book of Job is a classical treatment of this theme. A certain child's puzzlement over the question is expressive of much difficulty experienced among the wise and good. This child asked his mother, "Can God do anything?" The mother replied, "Yes, my dear." And then the child countered with a question which went to the heart of the philosophical and religious issue: "Then, why doesn't God kill the Devil?"

According to a naturalistic philosophy, evil is not a problem, but a fact. The opportunities for its appearance and operation are endless.

Perhaps the most elementary cause of evil lies in the fact that human beings live within a natural environment, which, while predominantly usable by them for their needs, does not operate primarily and specifically with reference to them. The readjustment of the earth's crust takes place in terms of the universe of physical stress and strain and without any consideration of the plans and purposes of men. If men choose to build a city on the lines of an active earth fault, a slip of several inches of the unstable portion of the earth's crust will cause great human loss and suffering and perhaps death to the persons who have built the city at that place. From their viewpoint the earthquake is an evil. From the standpoint of the physical factors involved, it is simply a readjustment of unstable portions of the earth's crust.

The relationship among the elements of the atmosphere, as effected by the impulses transmitted from solar and stellar space, represent a vast and intricate conjunction and change of forces which affect man's life both favorably and unfavorably. Without them he cannot live, but by them he sometimes dies. We speak of beneficent rains, destructive floods, killing drought, and when we do so the adjective applied represents only the human interest. In themselves, as part of a physical equation, the changes of the atmosphere have no value quality whatsoever, but as experienced by man they are given qualities of good and evil according to their effect upon his fortunes. By way of summary it may be said that a great deal of the evil in the world comes from physical phenomena which affect men unfavorably.

Another plane of experience in which evil arises is that of conflict among living organisms for the good which physical nature affords. Every living thing is seeking a place in which to live and the resources whereby to live. In many cases this means that one life preys upon another. The lion which finds human prey becomes classified among the categories of evil for mankind. The bacillus which finds a favorable environment in a human body for survival and multiplication is simply "making good" on its own account, but from man's viewpoint the ravages caused by disease germs are among the most destructive of all the evils he has to face. The list of evils which man experiences as the result of the natural expression of the life drive of lower organisms would be lengthy indeed.

Man also suffers a great deal of evil from the competition of his fellow humans. The strong and the intelligent prey upon the weak and dull. Organized powerful minorities exploit the weaker masses. Tribe and nation war against other tribes and nations. War has long been one of the greatest evils which have afflicted mankind. Indeed, there are many who are so impressed with the historical prevalence and present threat of war that they are pessimistic regarding the possibility of lessening appreciably the amount of evil in the world which wars may bring.

Another source of evil is the failure of the individual to manage his own life advantageously. Much of the evil which a man experiences is within himself. He fails to make the best of his hereditary bodily endowment and suffers from disease of his own fostering. He fails in controlling his appetites and breaks down his bodily balance through excess. He is unable to discipline his life according to the demands of his social environment. He is ill-adjusted with his fellows. He is unable to control his hates and fears and jealousies and to organize an integrated, constructive personality. He is out of step, friendless, uncoöperative. His mating is unsuccessful. His whole personal life is frustrated and unfruitful. Evil has captured the citadel of his existence.

Evil comes into human life also when the ties of love and loyalty which the individual has sent forth out of himself are broken. Friendships, family ties, the deepest personal attachments are interrupted by death through disease or accident. Men are compelled to give up in this way the dearest things they possess. Tragedy strikes into the individual life without order or reason. The young and promising and needed among human beings are often taken away.

It is clear that a realistic description of human

experience in its physical and social setting discloses an affrighting array of chances for evil. Some of it could be averted through the organization of better scientific and social controls and through the application of intelligence and right purpose in the management of individual lives. A certain amount of evil, however, would seem to be inevitable for human beings because of the cross tensions existing among a great number of factors which are coordinated on different planes or are in conflict on the same plane.

Evil becomes a problem, first, when the world is considered as a logical whole created and governed by an all-powerful and beneficent being, or secondly, when all experience is regarded as the embodiment and expression of an absolute mind, in which a logical and meaningful place must be found for every detail. Yet even in a world which is reduced to order and system by metaphysical formulas the incidents which the uninitiated would call evil obstinately persist as a part of human experience. They are not exorcised by the wand of the philosopher and theologian. Death, tragedy, disappointment, continue in a world supposed to be ordained according to divine and beneficent plan.

The older, pre-scientific view of the world and God's part in it, made God directly responsible for the evil under which man suffered. Storms, drought,

floods, earthquakes, wars, and pestilence were the
scourges of an angry God who by means of them
visited deserved punishment upon mankind for its
sins. Job's comforters tried to tell him that he had
had so much hard luck because he had unknowingly
sinned. The child in seventeenth century Massachu-
setts Bay Colony fell into a tub of water and
drowned because his father on the preceding Sunday
had done some farm work. Men were punished with
evil for their sins. But with all sins properly punished, there seemed to be a surplus of evil in man's
experience not otherwise accounted for. To meet this
factor evil was given a favorable evaluation as the
necessary trial to prove the individual's fitness for
eternal bliss. It was that by which man's moral quality was tested. It was a means of grace to those who
could meet and surmount it.

It must be admitted that, in more moderate
vein, a positive evaluation may justly be placed upon
the factor of evil. Human experience owes much of
its color and drive to the fact that not all is easy
sailing in life. Practical mastery over the physical
environment has been stimulated by grim necessity
and even scientific progress owes much, if not everything, to the prompting of a not-too-ready possession
of the means of existence. The evil which men have
suffered from their fellows has been the goad to the
development of laws and government. It is further

plain that the prized human qualities of fortitude, perseverance, patience, and heroism could never be found in an existence where there were no difficulties and no hazards.

However, to change the face of evil so completely as to make it seem all good, is likely to impress the modern man as casuistry, and, moreover, as casuistry which is lacking in sensitivity and in an even moderate regard for the testimony of experience. One cannot maintain one's respect for an all-knowing, all-powerful God who heaps such crazy excesses of suffering upon mankind. The formula breaks down with the overload which it is expected to carry. Add up all the suffering that has been in the world, through disasters of physical nature, through famine, wars, pestilence, disease, slavery, economic exploitation, miscarriage or denial of justice, physical weakness, mental inadequacy, and emotional maladjustment—add up this grand total and say that it represents the purpose and plan of a beneficent, omniscient, and omnipotent God! Such a God stands condemned either for his cruelty or his weakness.

There is, however, one is happy to say, a more intellectually satisfactory estimation of evil than the foregoing, which runs through the Judaeo-Christian literature and tradition. In its naive expression, this theory accepts an unresolved dualism in holding that there is an area of human experience which is ruled over by Satan, whose activities run counter to God's plans and purposes. And, apparently, God can do nothing about it. Against the waywardness of his creatures and the cruel indifference of nature, he seems to be powerless and to suffer with men on account of the sorrows which he cannot spare them. In a more philosophical statement this theory of the nature of evil is suggested in the Book of Job.

In that great drama devoted to an examination of the meaning of human loss and misfortune, the proposition that evil comes to men for their sins is suggested and refuted. Such a position is untenable, because evil is the portion of the just and the unjust alike. The earthly state of the godless may rival and even surpass that of the saint. The wicked man may enjoy health, wealth, and worldly acclaim to the end of his days. No, evil is something which, in the last analysis, cannot be associated with individual default. Evil comes into human lives as the impersonal resultant of the operations of nature as a whole. At the climax of the drama, the Voice out of the Whirlwind does not give to Job and his friends an explanation of evil, but instead opens the scroll of creation before them. Where were they when the foundations of the earth had been laid? Had they "commanded the morning" since their days began and "caused the dayspring to know its place"? Had they given thought to the operations of nature, which went forward without reference to the concerns of man—"to cause it to rain on a land where no man is"? Could they "bind the cluster of the Pleiades, or loose the bands of Orion"? Could they lift up their voice to the clouds that abundance of water might cover them? Had they considered the care of nature for the subhuman orders of living things, whereby the lioness knew how to hunt for its prey and the raven to find food for its young?

The Voice out of the Whirlwind offers no answer to the question which is raised in the Book of Job, but it gives it a new orientation. It views the fortunes of man *sub specie eternitatis,*—from the aspect of the totality of experience. Man is only a part of God's universe. He is only one manifestation of the universal operation of creative energy and of mechanical and organic adjustment. He is on the same basis as the wild ox and the eagle,—equipped to live as he can on what nature offers him. As a beneficiary of the universe, it is fitting that he should accept, along with its gifts, such conditions and limitations as are attached to them. The Voice of Nature speaks: "Who hath first given unto me, that I should repay him?"

It is a matter of high importance to come to terms with the nature of evil because upon such intellectual awareness all emotional reactions and adjustments to the vicissitudes of human life will be based. Evil is not to be ignored, to be denied, nor to be given a favorable guise as a necessary aspect of a perfect world made with special reference to man's enjoyment and destiny. Evil is a reality which must be faced, and the way in which the modern man faces it is in part a continuation of age-old attitudes, which are to be found within the Judaeo-Christian tradition, and in part a relative novelty, dependent on the use of modern scientific and social knowledge.

Against the most violent forces of nature man remains powerless, but there are many cases where science has been able to curb disastrous effects and turn to his advantage what might otherwise be inimical. He can dam up floodwaters and distribute them according to his needs. He can convey the otherwise wasted mountain moisture to make the desert productive. He can meet the menace of pestilence by applying his scientific knowledge to drain swamps, screen houses, destroy the hosts of disease germs and otherwise prevent the spread of the microscopic organisms which bring death and suffering. His knowledge of the economy of the human body can be applied to lighten or avert the ravages of individual illness and to insure better chances for favorable development to children. His application of practical skill and technical knowledge to industrial, extractive, and agricultural processes has progressed to the point at which the danger of famine and want can be discounted and the possibility of "an economy of abundance" begins to displace in the minds of imaginative and optimistic persons the restrictive categories of "an economy of scarcity." A new ideal of community life is satisfied with nothing short of a social order in which age-old evils of injustice, exploitation and individual defeat are eliminated in favor of a good life for all. Men even plan and labor today for a world in which that gigantic, human-made curse of war may be eliminated among nations which would be brought together in a coöperative search for the greater common good.

Man has taken arms against his "sea of troubles" and would "by striving end them." His attitude is no longer one of acceptance of all the ills that flesh has hitherto been heir to. Vast areas of experience have been removed from the category "will of God," once spoken with an air of pious resignation, and are now classified as the natural consequences of ignorance or self-indulgence. With increased knowledge has come a great sense of responsibility for avoiding or mitigating the evils of existence. Insofar as men and women take a hand in managing experience to the better ordering of their affairs and the lessening of the incidence of evil, they are taking over the traditional rôle of God and elevating the quality of their personal lives. In this matter of evil, educated, ethically sensitive, modern man has initiated a new and promising counter offensive.

And yet, when all that man can do has been done and will have been done, the fact remains that human life carries its load of tragedy, loss and sorrow. With what attitudes shall man meet the evil which is his inevitable lot? There is no new answer to this question. The older intellectual formula prompted the wise and good to say, "The Lord hath given and the Lord hath taken away; blessed be the name of the Lord!". Man bows before his fate and accepts it. His experience of sorrow is that of countless millions before him and will be the share of all who follow him. As he accepts the universe, so he accepts its conditions. But happily for us all, love and life are stronger than death. The hurt of cruel loss turns with time into the steady companionship of sustaining memory. The drive of continuing life brings new activities and new loyalties, with which it is possible to go on.

CHAPTER TEN

The Continuity and Progression of Goodness

MANY Christian theologians say with confidence that there can be no religious experience unless one believes in the eternal and absolute nature of truth and goodness—that there can be no devotion of oneself to human welfare unless one knows that all human fate is tied up with the conception of a divine creator who has put the moral element into man's life on earth out of his own moral perfection—that there can be no motive for the control of appetites and selfish passions except as man is considered a soul endowed by God with moral purposes. They are contemptuous of truth which exhibits the quality of change, adjustment, and development—of goodness which takes on new meanings in changed social environments. Truth and goodness, they hold, must be regarded as the same yesterday, today, and forever.

The difficulties raised by the theologian represent an inability to accept what are necessary positions of a naturalistic philosophy. For if one views experience from the standpoint of scientific description of what is and has been, it is inevitable that one should recognize the tentative, local, and developing quality of man's intellectual judgments and ethical evaluations.

As an illustration of the way in which man's intellectual formulas are changed and refined one may consider the progress which has taken place in man's description of the cosmos. From brute wonder and no intellectual explanation, to animistic and mythological stories accounting for the presence of nature and the operations of heavenly objects and earthly changes, to the early speculations of the first scientific age, to the maturing and more logical formulations of the Alexandrian period, to the reign for more than a thousand years of the earth-centered formulas of Ptolemy, to the sun-centered theory of Copernicus, to the mathematical-physical description of celestial phenomena provided by Isaac Newton, to the nebular hypothesis of La Place, to the current formulas of Einstein, Eddington, Jeans, and Millikan—that is the progression, roughly sketched, of man's intellectual explanation of the cosmos. Each of these levels of understanding was useful in its time. Each provided something of meaning and satisfied the desire to know and understand. Each in its turn became insecure and inadequate as knowledge was increased and the probing questions of the scientist were made more pointed and specific. Such elements of certainty as the earlier theory had provided were carried on into the later, but they were rearranged or reinterpreted in the system which superseded them. And so knowledge grows, piecemeal and experimentally. The satisfactory and useful intellectual formulas of yesterday are now outmoded, but they have had their part in the progressive reach for better and more adequate ones, which continually goes on. Truth changes. The truth of yesterday is the error of today, and today's truth will in turn be tomorrow's error. If there is any truth over and above the experimental and tentative advances of mankind toward understanding and control of experience, it ceases to be important for the scientific temper.

In the same way the concept of good has come to be associated with progressive success in the adventure of personal and social existence. Good as applied to the social life is a term which describes constructive and positive relationships among human beings. A good man is one who performs satisfactorily the functions expected of him as member of a family, as citizen, and as economic producer. The word good is also applied to his activities when they are socially useful and esteemed. Accordingly we should expect that different forms of social organization would exhibit varying examples of the good man and divergent estimations of the good action or quality. The primitive tribesman's set of social duties would be distinctive for his tribe. They might differ from those of a neighboring tribesman, and certainly in important particulars they will be seen as relatively immature when compared with those of a citizen of a city-state. In turn, the details of satisfactory performance of his social duties would be different for a citizen of a modern nation-state from the pattern of good civic functioning for a citizen of Athens, at 300 B.C. It may even be said that the last thirty years in the United States have provided decidedly different conceptions of what is good conduct, good policy, good attitude from what would have been so considered in 1900.

> "New occasions teach new duties; Time makes ancient good uncouth."

To take a single example of the progression of goodness, the change in the attitude toward respect for human life might be considered. Although our anthropological knowledge does not cover the case, it might be supposed that at one time there was no restriction upon killing any one who stood in one's way. The evolution of society to the stage of the tribe showed an advance over this general indifference to life to a point where it was demanded that the lives of fellow tribesmen should be respected. The commandment, "Thou shalt not kill," is a milestone in ethical evolution, but at first it applied particularly, and perhaps exclusively, to the members of the tribal group. Certainly the attitude of the Jewish God at the time such commandment was reputed to have been given to his people was as bloodthirsty as that of any Bedouin tribesman could have been toward the members of other tribes which were interfering with the realization of the purposes of his own.

With the development of larger patterns of social organization the obligation to respect the life of fellow citizen was enlarged, while with the extension of trade activities and friendly intercourse the prohibition of killing took on practically universal significance except in time of war. As the relationships of man in modern times have become more closeknit, there has been a progressive refinement of the conception both with respect to fellow citizen and others. Not mere abstention from lethal act as became the conception of good conduct, but the removal of conditions which lessened the vitality of an individual or indirectly resulted in his death. The cruelties of the penal code, the inadequacies of the purveyance of justice, the economic conditions which starve and stunt the human being, the prevalence of environments which blunt the moral sense and lower the quality of human experience, the human waste of war—all these have come to represent aspects of a new interpretation of the primitive admonition against the taking of life of a fellow tribesman. The concern for the life of others has ceased to be merely privative; it has become positive and constructive. The ethical demand is no longer the mere negative, "Thou shalt not kill," but it is a call to the reorganization of the community so that men may have more abundant life.

It might further be shown that a great many of the relationships among men which are evaluated in the terms of good and bad have likewise had a long history and shown similar development and refinement. We might name the relationship of state to citizen, of economic order to worker, of parent to child, of husband to wife, of employer to servant, of man to woman, of mankind to the lower animals, and in all of these we would see in the evolution through the centuries of man's past a continuity of meaning and a progression in the details of conduct through which that meaning was realized and expressed. Good is a growing concern.

Perhaps the critics of a naturalistic philosophy have been somewhat justified in their strictures because of the cautious, pedestrian application of their philosophy which the naturalists have made. The idealists have called the ethical doctrines of naturalism "hard-boiled," immediate, narrowly utilitarian. They have heaped contempt upon the statement that "a proposition is true because it works" and upon the ethical formula that "to be good a thing must be good for something." It is high time for the naturalist to take the offensive and declare the high significance of the fact that all the scientific and social controls which are operating in the world today and all the moral idealism which can be discovered in the hearts of men have evolved little by little in connection with the concrete experiences which called them forth.

The cautiousness of the philosophical naturalists may perhaps be understood if one considers the total situation against which they labored. Rationalistic and absolute philosophies were in possession. On their authority the conception of the perfect and unchanging nature of truth and goodness was dominant and was giving support and strength to an unyielding, unthinking *status quo* in all that concerned personal values and social institutions. The political and the economic systems in operation were right. The mores which governed personal relationships were given by divine inspiration or deduced from absolute and perfect models. A changing world was being strangled with formulas which denied the reality of change and made it impossible that the actualities of personal and social existence should be reëxamined and readjusted in the light of new circumstances. Accordingly the first emphasis of the naturalistic philosophy has been upon change, growth, the instrumental character of the intellectual processes, and the experimental quality of individual and social adjustments. The first necessity was to find a description of the processes of knowing and conduct which was consistent with the actual way in which human beings lived and social changes took place.

There can be no discounting the gains in sincerity and accuracy which result from the recognition of truth and goodness as relationships which occur and exist within experience, and there alone. There is grave danger, however, that the processes of truth-seeking and value-judging may be conceived in too particularistic fashion—as altogether individualistic, local, and immediate. No one solves an intellectual problem except in terms of his own past experience, but that experience is, in a very real sense, the product of the whole of human history. The practical arts and skills, the utensils and machines, and the science which one employs, are products of a long period of accumulation and elaboration. The body of social, ethical, and philosophical experience from which he judges a new situation has been prepared for him in a long and tumultuous past; it is the residue of forgotten struggle and heroism. Yes, the individual meets the problematic situation as something new. His decision in the case is novel and fateful. But he is not meeting his problem barehanded and alone.

If it is in the area of ethical judgments that the immediacy and particularism of the pragmatic or experimentalist philosophy has been most repellent to its critics, it is also there that the critics have had most to support them. There has been an emphasis in the naturalistic philosophy upon the act of choice in moral affairs which seems to cut the individual off from everything except his own interests. The naturalists have been so fearful of the power of habit and tradition that they seem to have isolated the individual from race experience altogether. They have not really, but at times they appear to have done so. They have emphasized problem solving to the point where no aspect of experience is stable and secure. They have drawn so far away from "indoctrination" that there remains nothing to be passed on or handed down. They have all but paralyzed parental responsibility and guidance in their enthusiasms for "child-initiated choice."

To the disadvantage of its total outlook the naturalistic philosophy to date has failed sufficiently to recognize and come to terms with the factor of continuity in human experience, and this failure has been particularly disastrous when it became a matter of discovering a religious orientation in a naturalistic world. The religious consciousness is not of a day, but of long time. The naturalist would hesitate to use the term "eternal verities" because of the connotation of rationalism which it carries, but he must know that goodness has a long history and that it is continuous with the evolution of social institutions and of ethical judgments. It is rooted in the past. The history of ethical values shows obstinate continuity as well as change and progression. Isaiah described the ideal community in which justice and peace should reign and wars should be no more, a long time before Professor John Dewey gave us his modern version of what a real community ought to be. And Jesus provided men with the formula for a rich and successful personal life in terms which substantially foretold the best advice of contemporary psychiatrists.

The fundamentals of good conduct were discovered long ago, and it is a needless impoverishment of the stock of human resources to lose hold on this fact. The early coalescence of individuals into social groups led thoughtful men of that distant era to assay the attitudes and forms of conduct which were suitable and favorable to the common welfare. As social patterns have become more extensive and complicated the same creative judgment with reference to what was fitting and good for individuals to do has developed and refined the primitive concepts. The whole wide sweep of historical development exhibits this recognition of ethical values and all the more mature formulations of social attitudes as found in the great historical religions and philosophies represent the funded and tested experience of mankind. Respect for the life and possessions of others, for the marriage relation, and for truth telling, are old and secure moral precepts. The modern scene calls for refinement and new application of them, but they represent the authoritative voice of experience no less now than some thousands of years ago.

In spite of the element of change and readjustment which is inevitable in moral relationships there is an abiding pattern of the good life in its larger outlines. Such change as is necessary in the light of new circumstances does not affect the spirit of the ancient concept. New moral structures are built upon the old foundations. The institutional change becomes necessary because the existent social forms miss the spirit of the social purpose which they originally embodied. In our own ethical-religious tradition the Deuteronomic Code was a social instrument designed to secure the greatest possible amount of human welfare under the conditions which it served. The cry of the later prophets of Israel was for social justice, which, though unrealized in practice, possessed the power of the ideal. And in our own day new prophets arise to recall us to the failure of our own time to realize the ancient spirit of justice and good.

There is among us, in the minds and hearts of us, a vision of social attitude and organization which has not been arrived at through processes of thinking and which is not subject to logical proof, but which exercises authority over us and influences our actions. It has come to us as a new growth on an old trunk, stimulated by the necessities of an industrial, nationalistic civilization and sustained by the new possibilities of human control provided by scientific knowledge. It is the vision of a society in which the material basis for the good life will be enjoyed by all—when children shall have the right food to eat and enough of it, when people shall live in decent and pleasant homes, and when the major financial anxieties of life will be taken care of by social foresight. Of a society in which differences of race, color, and religion will be merged in a common feeling of humanity. In which all socially useful work will be fairly esteemed and adequately rewarded. A vision of a world in which wars among nations will have come to an end forever.

There is also a pattern of personal self-management which is no less authoritative than our vision of a good community. It enjoins upon us the desirability and the advantage of making the most possible out of the physical endowment which we have inherited—of keeping well and vigorous. It demands of us that we should be *persons*, critically aware of our powers, creatively attached to the community in which we live, coöperative and constructive in our family and other human relationships, and, finally, serene and sure in our consciousness of an inner sincerity and integrity.

There *is* something in which we believe. There *is* a faith which we have in our own day. It is something bigger than our individual experiences, for it is the product of the experience of countless former generations and of the insight and aspirations of our own. It is something to hold to and to live by.

CHAPTER ELEVEN

As a Modern Man Lays Hold on Life

THE choice left to the modern man is not one between the old religion and no religion, for the necessity of finding an orientation to life and reality transcends the application of any particular intellectual instrument. Just as human beings had found and described for themselves satisfactory religious formulas before the rise of rationalistic philosophy, just so after the decline of that philosophy men discover new ways of understanding their place in the whole of experience. Following the confusion and dismay of seeing a traditional world in ruins, they are finding a new setting for their individual existences which day by day becomes more intelligible and more secure. The modern man has discovered a new way of envisaging himself in a new physical world as described by science, in a new social world as revealed by history and anthropology, and in a new world of the inner life which is presented to him by contemporary psychology. He has found a new way of laying hold on life.

In natural piety, he accepts the physical universe as the ground of his survival and welfare. He

sees himself as a product of the universal laboratory
—one of its latest and most gifted creations, subject
to the waywardness and the pains as well as the ad-
vantages which his powers bring with them, but
fitted to carry on with a measure, sometimes high
indeed, of efficiency and happiness. He is endowed
with the ability, apparently unique among living
things, of understanding to a degree the intricate
adjustments of physical and biological nature and of
standing in awe and reverence before them.

He finds his own and all human existence a
real and significant part of the universe. Mankind
for him is not a race of fallen angels, but of rising
primates, come from humble beginnings and on the
way to better things. He takes new confidence that
man may surmount his present difficulties from his
observation of what man has already done and he
experiences pride and gratitude as he looks back over
the long continuity of social evolution and is aware
of his indebtedness to all the generations which have
preceded him. His sympathy reaches out to grasp
the unity of mankind in his own day and to participate in the struggles which are going on the world
over for greater welfare, justice and security. More
specifically and poignantly he feels his membership
in the immediate community of which he is a con-
stituent and working part and is devoted to the
achievement of a more adequate society in which the

individual citizens may be respected and well adjusted as persons and provided with the material means to the good life.

Is it not striking that there is nothing particularly new about this so-called "new world outlook"? Is it not identical with the insights and aspirations of the choicest spirits of a large part of the world for a long, long time? Saints and sages have proclaimed it, and prophets have thundered it as their message to renegade and stiffnecked generations. All of which suggests the thought that this way of laying hold upon life is older than any particular descriptions of the natural order or any specific form of philosophic invention. Such a fact further suggests that the rationalistic philosophy with which the Western man's world view and his ethical aspirations have been tied up so closely is only an episode or incident in a form and process of life adjustment which is older and more fundamental than it by far.

An important characteristic of the new religious orientation is its directness, or its immediacy. Such a religion consists exactly and alone of the attitudes which enter into it and the acts which those attitudes engender. In connection with it there are no ulterior rewards. There is no delayed realization of values. The attitude, the act, the way of life, are good in themselves—the best there is, in fact, to which everything is to be subordinated and, if need be, sacrificed.

In this directness and immediacy of experience there may be elements of superiority over a religion which rests upon mythological or rationalistic formulas. The difficulties and disadvantages of a religion established on such foundations are multiplied when it holds out the promise of compensation for the ills of this life in a world to come. Where general and abstract principles are accepted in advance of concrete experience they remain to be made specific and concrete. God says, "Love your fellow man" and the believer may try to follow the divine command, but there is no guarantee that the acceptance of a universal mandate will ever eventuate in the individual life in terms of philanthropy or of enthusiasm for improving the lot of human beings. There is the further danger that the abstraction will remain separate from the needs and reality of everyday experience, and thus will bind upon the backs of men and women burdens too heavy to be borne. With regard to the factor of other-worldness, it will be recognized that any religion which takes account of a life after death in which goodness done here will be rewarded and evil done here will be punished, sets up a dangerous machinery of refined and disguised selfishness. Attention and interest inevitably come to be centered on the objective and external reward of goodness instead of on the living experience of charity and constructive social acts.

The new world-and-life orientation which is operating in the lives of so many men and women of this generation, and which we have called by the name of religion, is universal in its scope. It reproduces the best spiritual insight of so many cultures that it could well be taken as the continuation and flowering of each and all. Followers of many historical religions might identify its principles with the deepest insight and the highest moral values of their own religion and recognize the new and universal phase as the modern and completed realization of ancient sacred truth and aspiration. And thus would disappear one of the most potent sources of hate and strife and bloodshed which has ever operated among the sons of men!

It is further significant that the social attitudes and values of the new religion represent an appropriate foundation for the realization of peace and coöperation among the nations of the world and for the internal reconstruction of national communities. Between these two aspects of social improvement there is no necessary contradiction. The attitudes and the social practices which are appropriate to the realization of the good national community are neither limited nor exclusive. They run over national boundaries. They provide the key to the welfare of the nations of the world considered collectively just as they do for the improvement of conditions within each nation. Neighbor can be spoken among nations as it can be among nationals.

In a very real sense, given constructive attitudes on international relationships, there is great advantage, even necessity, in the present national system of political organization. The work of community building must have a locus. It must be organized and administered in units large enough to develop power and provide resources, and not so large as to be unwieldy and as to fail to catch the imagination and stir the loyalty of individuals. Enthusiasm and devotion to the community ideal can be engendered on a national scale and according to a national pattern without coming into conflict with those larger loyalties to the international good which preserve, in a worldwide sweep, the most comprehensive conditions of human welfare.

As for the internal reconstruction of community living, what meaning the new ethical evaluations and attitudes carry!

To respect and foster every citizen without reference to race, color, or religious belief;
To apply twentieth century science to create the material resources of the good life;

To distribute those resources in generous and constructive ways;

To improve the administration of the civil government for honest and efficient social service;

To place the courts and the judicial system at the impartial command of all;

To expand and improve the means of education so that individuals may learn and practice the principle of social-minded conduct, and so that the gifts and abilities of each may be developed and placed at the service of an appreciative society;

To provide the means of wholesome recreation for all;

To make of every home a creative environment where children, loved and wanted, may be guided wisely and sympathetically to sound maturity,—

there is the greatest challenge to men of good will which has ever been issued in the history of the world.

In this book an effort has been made to describe a pattern of belief—a system of loyalties and long-range purposes—a way of laying hold on life, which seems to be not only consistent with the intellectual demands of our generation, but representative of its best ethical insight. What has been presented is a report of experiences which can be identified within the minds and hearts of living persons and for which no word except religion seems to be an adequate name.

Among such persons there are many whose intellectual outlook is such that they can say no good word for religion, associating it as they do with certain specific formularies of belief and certain systems of value which they cannot accept. Perhaps they will resent having their experience classified under that name. On the other hand, there are many whose intellectual necessities do not compel them to come so completely to terms with the methods of science as this work has done. They are nevertheless in the forefront of the ethical advance of our day, and the moral values which they live by and propagate represent the most sensitive insight of this generation. This group see themselves as finding their way back to the inspired teachings of the prophets of Israel and preëminently to the way of life of Jesus. But whether in the name of God and for the realization of his kingdom or in the name of humanity seeking the ideal of the good community, an ethical and religious revolution of major scope and power is under way among us.